WE WERE THE PERFECT PAIR, BUT YOU DIED.

WHAT DO I DO NOW?

I0141434

JOHN LESLIE

A LOVE STORY

The *little* RedHen BOOK GROUP

Little Red Hen Book Group
Spring, Texas

ISBN: 978-0-615-87380-0
Printed in the United States of America
Little Red Hen Book.
First printing August 2013

The book's cover is by Ron Folsom, who also was responsible for the layout of the pages of this book. Ron continues to partner with John (this is their fourth book together). They both are senior citizens who share an interest in the issues associated with aging.

ALSO BY JOHN LESLIE

Book of Toasts
I'm Getting Older, But I'm Not Dead Yet!
Words, Some Wise, Some Otherwise
Make Your Aging Memory Sharp As A Tack!
Itinerant Preacher
The Leslie Family
Grandmothers
The Scottish Leslie's (a compilation)

LECTURE SERIES

Cowboys, Indians and Presbyterians
Caveman, Rabbit Stew and Jesus
Preparing for the End of Life
Dancing with Doctors

ABOUT THE AUTHOR

WITH THIS BOOK, "What Do I Do Now?", John Leslie continues his quest to write about contemporary moral issues relating to living and dying, both topics of interest to aging Americans. This fourth book in this series discusses many of the dilemmas facing a relatively young survivor of a marriage which ended with the death of a partner.

The first book of the present-day series, "Little Book of Toasts", celebrated the joy of life.

His second book, "I'm Not Dead Yet", was a guide for seniors who wished to prepare for the period after their death and covered contemporary morality and ethical issues. He lectures on the topics of this book in his series, "Preparing for The End of Life".

His third book, "Words, Some Wise, Some Otherwise", is about the words we use to make life meaningful. Luckily, there are times in our journey when we just want to "lay back" and enjoy life. "Words" is that kind of book.

He now is addressing the major fear of every aging person: loss of memory. His book, "How to Make Your Aging Memory Sharp As A Tack!" will be published in 2014.

John and his wife, Janice, reside in Houston, Texas.

PREFACE

THIS IS A LOVE STORY.

Many happy moments preceded a couple's losing struggle with disease. Following the arrival of an illness that could not be cured, there is watchful waiting, followed by loving care, and, finally, acceptance that death is inevitable.

Then there's death itself. Trauma, grief, and depression follow. Waiting in the wings and then coming in without an invitation are remorse and unnecessary guilt.

The death of a longtime companion ends a happy partnership. It's not something that can be prepared for, even though it is anticipated.

This love story has no ending. The path to recovery is painful and takes a long time. Friends, therapy, hard work, prayer, and luck—all have their place in the journey. That new love is possible is a pleasant surprise, sometimes not sought after, and sometimes wanted but impossible to find.

Every now and then, there's a happy ending.

This is that story.

This work is dedicated to those remaining after their companion has died.

I hope this book helps.

Profits from the sales of this book will be donated to the American Cancer Society

TABLE OF CONTENTS

INTRODUCTION

THIS BOOK IS a story about the ending of a life and the surviving companion starting over.

Finding the answer to the question, "What do I do now that my partner has died?" is unique for every person. If you've read my other books, you'll recognize some of the issues described in those books that are being handled in this one. This is not just one person's story; it was from the accounts of many persons that this book emerged.

You'll be an observor of events in the life of a survivor whose life partner died from cancer and who struggles to live on. The chronicle starts in the uneventful, but happy, marriage of a couple. Their lives begin falling apart as death begins its relentless and unstoppable march.

In a sense, this is a "gender neutral" story. The emotions and happenings to a survivor are not exclusive to one gender or another. However, this survivor's story is about a woman.

The book's chapters disjointedly follow the natural course of events. Death is like that. It is not orderly; it's erratic, cruel, insensitive, painful, and can't be controlled. Eventually, the chaos ends and a semblance of normalcy returns. For some, normalcy doesn't occur for a long, long time.

I imagine we all like to think, if given the chance for before-death planning, death would be better handled. It would. It's overwhelming, the trauma of sickness, followed by death and the demands made on survivors.

Knowledge's gift is a calming and comforting enabler for both the dying and survivors. The pain, suffering, and distress that death creates are companions, but not friends. Regardless of what could have been, death has to be dealt with.

There is no "do over."

I Didn't Want To
Lose You

MY STORY STARTED years ago. I met you, fell in love, and married. We bought a house; children followed, along with job changes and moves to different cities...pretty much the typical story of an average, happily married couple.

We had the same problems our friends had. There was never enough money; the kids misbehaved; the car broke down and needed repairs we couldn't afford. The credit card was always the last resort at the end of the month; the month always seemed to last longer than the money.

It was a great life.

We often talked about our marriage and how lucky we were to have found one another. And we had so many wonderful, caring friends. It was a great life. We were the perfect pair.

But something happened.

You died.

On that clear, cold morning, in the warmth of our bedroom, I was stabbed with the pain of accepting that sometimes there isn't any more. It's over.

No more hugs, no more memorable moments to celebrate together, no more phone calls just to chat, no more "Just one minute." No more cuddling together for the fun of it. No more watching for that look in your eyes that said, "Tonight's the night." No more silly presents to celebrate a birthday or an anniversary. No more.

Sometimes, what you care about the most gets all used up and goes away...never to return. It can happen before you can say good-bye, before you say again, "I love you." I discovered there's never enough time.

I found it amazing that a typical, average marriage could be so easily destroyed. It didn't take very long, either.

Since your death, I've thought so many times about how wonderful it would be to have another chance. What I wouldn't give to have another opportunity to take advantage of all the things that came to mind when I was miserable with grief. I've wished I could have followed my mother's advice: "While you have it, it's best you love it...and care for it...fix it when it's broken...and heal it when it's sick." At the time she said it, I didn't know that advice wouldn't work for a husband with terminal cancer.

Wouldn't it be great to have another chance for a marriage, for the two of you to worry together about an old car that needs work, or children with bad report cards, or dogs with arthritic hips, and aging parents and grandparents?

Wouldn't it be great to have another chance to share together the events which brought joy? Like holding a baby, hugging your school-bound youngster, watching as your graduating daughter dresses for the senior prom, and the thrill of feeling the soft skin of your grandchild's face?

I'm trying to accept that things happen that prevent sharing life's pleasures with your partner. I'm trying to learn to live and accept life's joys...alone. I search for some measure of joy.

It's difficult; joy is illusive for me now. Sometimes I think it's impossible to attain.

Too late, when there's nothing you can do, you want to keep your partner and share memories and make new ones because he is worth it. You want to because you are worth it.

I didn't want to lose you. But I did. It's very pleasant remembering the good times — those wonderful moments we had together. However, for some reason, the things I wished for when you were so ill keep interrupting my thoughts. All kinds of events run through my head. There are times when I can shut off the pain for a moment. When I do, I give myself the luxury of remembering better times. There are lots of good memories. For instance, I smile to myself thinking about those fancy, big events your company put on each year. We thought they were so unimportant, but we had so much fun. I can't control the things I think of; they just come spilling out.

There were lots of funny stories. And our love affair was out of a storybook. Our marriage...it didn't last long enough.

There were the silly arguments, the wonderful make-ups, vacations, children, in-laws, friends, church, time for just the two of us in restaurants, fast food takeout, nights curled up on the sofa with a good book, standing naked in front of you, filled with anticipation. I could go on and on listing the things that made me want to keep you. I cherish those memories. And then, no matter how hard I try to keep the good memories in my head, the pain that had been chased away with pleasant memories, returns.

I don't know when I realized we can't take the things which make us happy and isolate them from the things that make us sad...or sorry. Maybe it was just something that I learned as I grew older. Good and bad are mixed together.

Oh, how I've wanted to ignore the painful memories. But I can't. Knowing the thoughts are inseparable isn't helpful, and it's not healing either.

As I begin my life without you, there are people, things, and memories that are special. I'll keep them as close as I can for as long as I can. And, if I'm able, my new life will eventually enable me to lose the intensity of the painful and sad memories. However, there are times now when the weight of the past just wears me down.

I didn't want to lose you, but I did. Remembering you is a memory that's at the top of any list I make.

CHAPTER 2

THE DIAGNOSIS

WHEN YOU'RE NOT young, but not old, what are you?

Dead? I've tried to convince myself there's something else. But I can't.

It's relatively easy to divide life into pieces like young, middle aged, and old and then look back and let events define the piece of life where you were at such and such time. There's a point where you say, "Yes, I'm in the middle part of life," and accept that youth has passed you by. Wrinkles start showing up, stomach muscles relax, desserts taste better than vegetables, walking is easier than running, wine tastes better than water, dinner out is lots better than fixing a meal. The "middle part of life" is great and I wish it would last forever.

However, unexpected bad news creates a new definition of your piece of life. In my case, the problems that go along with this new period very quickly became the "not-so-good" period. In fact, the piece of life I'm remembering now is a horrible period from hell.

When your illness was raging through your body, and you were incapable of talking to me, I imagined life without you. When that terrible thought overtook me, it was so scary that for a little while I found life undefinable. But when (usually after a good cry) the shock was slightly overcome, I tried again to visualize a future without you. The images I came up with were catastrophic. I imagined the worst of every scenario. Does a time of pain and suffering have to be defined? I hope not, because I couldn't do it.

I thought I could (and I did) easily handle your illness when there was a possibility you would be cured. But when we heard the news that you were in the very last part of life, I fell apart. It was emotionally draining, knowing you were not in a temporary phase that would eventually pass. With acceptance of your imminent death, life took a different, dramatic turn. You were going to die...soon. Realizing there's an ending you can't control is a frightening experience. Knowing impending death was taking over our lives was a terrible divider. I hated that knowledge then. I still hate it.

For my husband, life didn't divide itself into many different parts. He didn't have time. If only his life could have had a beginning, a middle and a very long final part. He skipped too much of life. The very last part came too, too fast and didn't last nearly long enough.

Our family doctor made the initial cancer diagnosis. He picked up the clues during a routine medical exam.

The doctor's diagnosis made us agonizingly aware there was a possibility your life would end way before either of us was ready. We learned that, even if doctors could put the illness at bay for a while (and they tried), the threat was always out there, lurking somewhere in your body. The fear held us hostage. It wouldn't go away.

They have wonderful cancer treatments these days. We tried to find one; we looked for something that would give you five, 10, or 15 more years. We searched for a miracle; even a small miracle would have been wonderful. While we explored options, there was always in the back of our minds the nagging question, "If, some way, we get 'it' stopped in its tracks, would 'it' return?"

As the cancer continued its spread through your body, we anxiously read everything we could about new treatments. Our hopes soared with every new development, every potential medical advance announced on TV or in the paper. It's not fair: trying to find a treatment that worked, but at the same time wondering if the cancer will return even if the present cancer is eliminated. No matter whether on-going treatment will be through surgery, radiation, or chemotherapy, the threat of a recurring cancer is always lurking in the background. So, when you start with hope and subtract from it stress, fear, and pain, what's left is not enough time.

We may have mistakenly obsessed over the possible return of the disease; curing the present cancer was our major goal.

We couldn't escape wishing for a cure. We couldn't escape the anxiety that a cure might not come in time, or that a new treatment would be announced too late for you. We prayed for a cure; that failing, we prayed for remission. Even with the possibility of remission, the threat of the disease's return hung over our heads. And we agreed the fear of a return would be a threat the rest of our lives, an albatross to both of us....

But I'm getting ahead of the story.

When the very real possibility of death enters the life cycle sooner than you ever thought it would, events move along a path that's been laid out and described by other persons who have gone through exactly what is now always on our mind. But it's an original, terrifying event to us.

Doctors know, too, about the steps in the journey. However, we were lost; we had never gone down a road like this before. We didn't believe the stories we heard. In our minds your disease was special, different from the others. We thought about our parents; except for my mother, the others had been dead for many years. We could take nothing away from remembering their deaths that was any help in our present situation.

The dying process creates so many emotions. I've yelled at it, cursed it, doubted God because of it, and prayed for forgiveness because of it. I don't think there's anything out there that wasn't considered if we thought there was a possibility it would do some good. We discussed some really goofy ideas. We were desperate.

As the shock of your illness began to settle in, we agonized over cancer's advance through your body. We anticipated the possibility of remission. As a process out of our control, we mistakenly assumed medical science would work a miracle. It does...for some people. But science didn't work its magic for us.

It takes cancer time to become a killer. Sometimes it silently works in the body a long, long time before it announces itself. The disease moves, without pain, faster in some persons than others. We found out you had cancer when it was in Stage 4, a bad time to think of remission. You had no awareness of it being in your body through the three early stages. When we learned you were in serious trouble, it seemed the disease was speeding along in your body at an "Indianapolis Speedway" clip. Too, too fast.

Without successful treatment, a cancer victim goes from one declining stage to another, each a little worse than the one before. Sometimes the movement from one phase to the next occurs without an announcement. It's both a physical and a mental thing. Whether you know it or not, you carry the baggage from each previous phase into the next.

It's like skipping on a sidewalk hopscotch course: sometimes you can jump right through, stepping in the middle of each square. At other times, you step on the chalk line. Your progress to that point ends. You start the next game with a penalty. I called the phases you were going through, "Hopscotch to Dying." It wasn't funny; it was a way for me to cope. If, while hopping through the squares in either direction, the player steps on a line, misses a square, loses balance, or is unable to pick up the marker, the turn ends. You skip into the next phase of dying carrying the score from the previous game because prior mistakes are not left behind. Seldom does a person with two penalties or more win the game.

Gross? Yes. It was a coping method for me.

Sometimes it seemed your "hop" turned from a skip into a fast skip, until, finally, the cancer took over your body, racing through the Hopscotch's course, touching every forbidden line. I know now how each phase of cancer progresses through the body, but I learned about it late in your life. It was a challenge I couldn't participate in and a competition you couldn't win. I wasn't the victim, you were. But both of us were involved in the process. It was terrible.

It hurts to think about the advance of your disease. It seemed to happen so easily. As I said, I was a spectator. At its beginning, neither of us knew something terrible was happening to you. The first sign wasn't noticed. You experienced no pain. Without a medical examination, there was no way you could have known there was something inside your body that would eventually kill you. It's possible an exam wouldn't have caught it early on.

When did it start? Who knows? It could have been something you got from your dad or mother at your birth. They had no idea that they were giving you a terrible "gift." Luckily, for them, they weren't around when you found out.

It could have come from your heritage, the workplace or an allergy...its origin would never be known.

You became a victim of a killer disease. There was no crime; the police couldn't arrest anybody. The doctors and scientists solved a piece of the puzzle; they told us the name of the cancer that was taking you away from us. Their medical experiences enabled them eventually to diagnose your cancer. But they weren't so hot at curing it.

With some people, doctors can cut the problem out, or kill it with radiation or chemicals. Sometimes, when the awareness of cancer comes too late and this was your case, all they can do is manage the pain, and, maybe, slow the progress of the disease a little.

All the survival statistics in the world don't mean a thing when it's too late. There were bunches of cancer cells throughout your body. The doctor said the initial issue was colon cancer, but it didn't make any difference now. The disease had spread everywhere. It took charge of your body.

Our primary care doctor was one we had used for years; we knew him well enough to have cocktails with occasionally. We even discussed politics with him. We had a lot of confidence in his medical skills.

He didn't have the courage to say it.

I did, but to myself. You were going to die.

CHAPTER 3

THAT
"DAMNED DIAGNOSIS Ride."

I'LL NEVER FORGET the trip home from the doctor's office. It was right after we officially became aware you had cancer. We didn't know yet how serious it was, or what would be happening, nor how soon.

We later referred to the trip as that "Damned Diagnosis Ride." The doctor told us the tests indicated a Stage 4a cancer and that treatments should start as soon as possible. He avoided the answer to the unasked question, "How long do I have to live?" We didn't have the nerve to ask.

When he said, "You should begin getting your affairs in order," our legs felt like rubber. If we weren't already seated, we would have collapsed.

We didn't talk as we walked to where our car was parked. You paid the parking fee and drove out onto the street, still silent. It was not until we were on the freeway, headed home, that you said, "I don't feel sick. I'm still doing the things I've done all my adult life. How can I feel good and still have cancer?"

Silence.

And then the dam broke. You started venting about doctors doing things just to make more money, about the poor training doctors were getting these days, about how a lot of them can't even speak English. And then you went on about how long you have to wait to see a doctor even though you ar-

rive at his office before your appointment time, about all the unnecessary tests they make you take, and more things than I can
remember. I even think you said something about the whole
scheme was a Democratic plot because you gave money to the
Republican Party.

It's fair to say you were in denial of the doctor's diagnosis. There was no doubt about it. It was denial.

You said, "That doctor is crazy. I don't have cancer. They
probably got my test results mixed up with some other poor
soul's. I exercise regularly. I feel good. I don't drink excessively.
I don't smoke. I don't have any bad habits. No other person in
my family has ever had cancer. It's not me. I don't have cancer."

After what I thought was a reasonable pause, I said the
only thing that seemed appropriate, "Let's get a second opin-
ion."

Silence. This time the silence was really ominous.

I didn't know it at the time, but you were in the beginning of what I've since learned is the first of the stages of dying:
Denial. I recognized the "denial" part; I just didn't know it was
part of a process. When you first expressed your belief, no, it
was hope, that your diagnosis was a mistake, I thought to myself, "Wouldn't it be wonderful if we found out you really didn't
have cancer, that a mistake was made somewhere?"

When we got home, the first thing you did was open a
Coke; no booze. Then you popped yourself down in your recliner. You didn't turn on the TV. You just sat.

Out in the kitchen, I could hear you mumbling to yourself. The words weren't discernible, but I imagined you were giving yourself a pep talk by thinking the doctor had made a mistake, a BIG mistake. You didn't have cancer!

We didn't talk about the diagnosis any more that day. The atmosphere was strained. There was a big, black cloud in our house. But, in the evening, you did ask if I had made an appointment with an oncologist. I had. Unfortunately, our appointment was 10 days into the future.

We tried ignoring the cancer possibility. Then we started asking questions. We Googled cancer. We Binged cancer. We tried talking to a few close friends. I think we would have waved down passing cars if the strangers within them could authoritatively say, "You don't have cancer." In our research we did find out that your type cancer developed and spread quickly and destructively. The literature reported persons in your advanced stage of cancer have only a small chance of surviving more than five years.

The 10 days before we saw the doctor were a blur. Each day was worse than the preceding one. We were scared to death. My mind imagined all sorts of things, all bad. I thought you must be in a living hell, tormented by doubt and fear.

The visit with the oncologist didn't go well. Our appointment time had come and passed by about an hour, and we were still sitting in the waiting room. We should be used to waiting... every doctor's appointment time was a bad approximation. However, this time the delay caused the smoldering emotions from that "Damned Diagnosis Ride" to rise to the surface. You were a bundle of nerves; all of them stretched to the breaking point.

Finally, the right name was called: yours. When the nurse asked you to step on the scale so that your current weight could be put into your file, you snapped, "My weight is not what I came here for. I can get weighed any place, even at the circus." But you stepped onto the scale. I noticed you didn't look to see how much you weighed. I did. You were losing weight.

Luckily, the nurse was experienced; she didn't say anything in response to your complaint. She just wrote the numbers down and then showed you into the examining room.

I came along. One thing everybody had told us was that four ears were better than two. I also brought along a notebook, convinced that having a medical diary was a good thing to have, both now and in the future. I wished I had started one years ago; that might have given us some insight into this terrible mess we're in. But maybe not.

I had written down questions we wanted to ask, and I planned to write what the doctor said so we would have a good recollection of the visit. I didn't write anything in the book. When the doctor started talking, I was so depressed at his words that my hands stayed in my lap, each hand gripping the other. The doctor confirmed the earlier diagnosis and then concluded with the words, "You need to think about getting your affairs in order." This was the second doctor to tell us that.

It isn't necessary to say anything more about this doctor's visit. It took a few days, but we got the laboratory's confirmation of the first physician's diagnosis. It was cancer. And it was in an advanced stage.

You were dying. And you would die within a short, too short, time. There were some treatments that would slow the spread of the disease a little, but not much. We discovered there was only a small difference in the survival rate between Stage 4a and Stage 4b. The difference didn't give us any hope.

They told us they would manage the pain (thank God for that!). We didn't think about it at the time, but later it became evident that advancements in pain management were truly a blessing. As your cancer progressed, you suffered a lot, but not as much as you would have if those wonderful drugs weren't available.

CHAPTER 4

ANGER

YOU STARTED LOOKING for someone to blame. What else could you do?

You were mad; you said surely this illness was caused by something your parents had done to you or something I had done to you, or something the water company had put in the water, or atom bomb testing. Anyone you could take out your anger on was fair game. You were continuing your tirade against unknown causes as your list continued to expand.

Although you were angry, I was yet to see your real anger.

It's one thing to try to convince yourself that the doctors were wrong. And you did try. You told me that the time came when your denials began to fade and you accepted that something was seriously wrong, that there were changes going on in your body over which you had no control. You were the kind of person that couldn't tolerate indecision or ignorance; but both these traits were now present in your life.

You knew you were dying but not when you would die.

You knew there were things the doctors could do to slow the cancer's onslaught, but not whether the radical treatments would be worth the price to mind and body.

What a mess.

I couldn't pinpoint when your "anger" began manifesting itself.

You started raising your voice when you talked; you shouted too. Why raising your voice was important to you, I'll never know. I even heard you utter a few curse words that I hadn't heard since I was a teenager. You were angry.

I watched your face during one of your episodes. Your complexion changed; it went from slightly tan to hot red. Little beads of perspiration broke out on your forehead. I thought at the time that steam was going to shoot out your ears, but that didn't happen, of course.

Almost instantly after one of your tantrums, you realized you were behaving uncharacteristically bad, and got this funny look. Your mouth turned down, your shoulders slumped, head bowed, and you just stood in place for a few seconds. I'm sure you wanted to say, "I'm sorry," but you just couldn't do it. Instead, you did a 90-degree turn and stomped out of the room. Incidentally, the room was still smoking from your use of gutter words.

This "anger" emotion was not helpful. With terminal cancer, you're not in control of your life anymore. I remember when I accepted that the cancer you had would kill you. I heard the doctors say it, in their own way, but it was a terrible moment when I truly permitted myself to acknowledge that your time on earth was now controlled by something we had no control over.

I was angry, too. But it didn't change anything. Besides, I had to keep my anger hidden. It makes no difference that the doctor said there were treatments that could extend your life. We considered trying them all because you're a fighter. However, after a while, you decided not to try any of them. You concluded you'd rather have a few good months rather than having to fight through treatments that would delay the final result for a little while. You said over and over that, at this stage, quality of life was important.

You had decided to die.

Neither of us had any idea that your death would be sooner than either of us imagined. We were hoping for a year. We missed that target substantially.

No one tried to argue with you about what caused your cancer. What good would it do? After a while, anger didn't help either. There were continuing conversations about taking treatments that, hopefully, would extend your life. But you were characteristically stubborn. You wouldn't change your mind, so after a while, I stopped bringing up the subject.

In the past, reading the Bible was something you did occasionally, mostly in preparation for a Sunday School Class. You often jokingly said the pages of the Bible were the best cure for insomnia you knew of. After your diagnosis, especially during this anger phase, you spent hours reading the Bible. I guess you were looking for hope and thought that maybe you'd find it in the Bible. Or find a miracle.

For some inexplicable reason, you discovered a Bible verse we agreed fit your condition. It's from the 38th chapter of Isaiah:

> *At that time, Hezekiah got sick. He was about to die. The prophet Isaiah, son of Amos, visited him and said, God says, "Prepare your affairs and your family. This is it: You're going to die. You're not going to get well."*
>
> *Hezekiah turned away from Isaiah and, facing the wall, prayed to God: "God, please, I beg you: Remember how I've lived my life. I've lived faithfully in your presence, lived out of a heart that was totally yours. You've seen how I've lived, the good that I have done." And Hezekiah wept as he prayed painful tears.*
>
> *Then God told Isaiah, "Go and speak with Hezekiah. Give him this message from me, God, the God of your ancestor David: 'I've heard your prayer. I have seen your tears. Here's what I'll do: I'll add fifteen years to your life. And I'll save both you and this city from the King of Assyria. I have my hand on this city.'"*
>
> *(From the Eugene Peterson version of the Bible)*

Talk about luck. Could we figure out how to get that kind of commitment from God? Fifteen more years! Did we know anyone who could get a commitment like that from God? I didn't. I hadn't prayed to God recently, and I was afraid to try. I finally did it. I prayed. I prayed a lot.

God and I didn't talk, but I didn't give up hope.

Somebody surely does talk to God on a regular basis. I needed to find that person. Maybe the two of them (that's God and the advocate person) could work out something. A miracle would be nice.

I couldn't find anyone who performed miracles. You and I talked about it and concluded we'd have to make our own miracle.

We couldn't.

I imagine everyone tries to anticipate what will happen in the future.

I haven't yet met anyone who can guarantee the events of the future will play out as we wish. When a person has been told they have cancer and might die, the first response is usually denial. Denial means the people who said you have cancer are wrong. (After saying the word, "wrong," slam your fist on the table! That makes the point more real.)

The second significant event in the struggle is anger. I thought we had already gone through the anger stage in the period right after we got the diagnosis. I was wrong. There were many more episodes of slamming your hand on the table; there were also a few broken pieces of furniture.

The reality of right now, the present, is the closest to an event we can almost control. Anger fits right into the present. The anger you were experiencing was much more real than faded remembrances of the past. Luckily, over time, the past is glossed over and memories of unpleasant events fade.

What will happen in a very short upcoming period is pretty close to anticipating and predicting the future. Only for a moment can you gain insight to the next moment. Your anger moved from one event to the next, almost out of control. You said that, with anger, you got the illusory feeling you were in charge...for a little while. Unfortunately, while your emotions were still raging, you re-discovered a truth you knew: anger couldn't make your cancer go away.

Getting upset was not your typical response to a problem. Your style up to now had been "cool, calm, and collected."

I was angry, too, because I was incapable of controlling my husband's life-ending emotions. My husband could have won a prize for anger, if someone were giving one. Like mine, your anger was ineffective.

How does "right now" relate to anger? It's the reality of a dangerous emotion. When you're really mad at something and you can't change the event, but you want to—that's when responses can be downright foolish and, sometimes, hurtful. The way a person displays anger is often very embarrassing when viewed in hindsight. Humiliating may be a better word.

We both had plenty of anger...and humiliation.

Learning cancer is taking over your body and the strong likelihood of death seemed to be enough reason for you to be angry. Your first emotion was denial, but you've now gone beyond that. You've been blindsided. Something snuck up on you and WHAM! You've finally convinced yourself they didn't make a mistake with the diagnosis, so denial wouldn't work anymore. So you decided to get mad at something or somebody for letting this thing happen to you.

Anger! You've earned the right to be angry! Don't waste the emotion. Don't throw away this precious moment of reality because you think a future time will be better. Getting angry seems right.

Someone should have told me: Be careful.

I learned that anger is an emotion characterized by antagonism toward someone or something you feel has deliberately done you wrong. You questioned who gave you cancer? Get angry towards them. You don't know who it was? Try something else, like feeling angry at your pain, your fear, your confusion. Though it didn't seem so at the time, we later decided anger is a good thing as you go through the emotions of coming to grips with dying. It's a way to express negative feelings.

However, excessive anger can cause an increase in your blood pressure and other physical changes that make it difficult to think straight. And sometimes you get angry with the people you love the most.

Here's that admonition again: Be careful..

We both felt a need to get help managing this raw emotion. Who? I discussed your illness and its consequences with our adult children. They were mystified, too. Frightened, with no ability to empathize with your pain, they didn't have any suggestions.

With the preliminaries of denial out of the way, you had made good friends with anger. You were mad! At this early stage, anger seems to be lying in wait whenever you experienced the increasingly familiar emotions of discomfort, pain, boredom, confusion, embarrassment, fear or worry. Everything made you angry.

You were not much fun to be around while you were in this funky stage. You eventually shifted to a stronger emotion (maybe it was guilt, or regret, or envy. I never was able to identify the emotion). I suppose you thought these more "expressive" emotions would allow you to step through the fear you were experiencing. Most often, the "kickback" was more anger! We learned, as your cancer progressed, we couldn't even control the present. (We used to think the present was the one thing we could control. Stupid us.)

A doctor told me it's OK to feel anger (or did I read that in the Reader's Digest? Or did someone say it when I was talking to a couple of our neighbors?). Anyway, I decided it's OK to feel a strong emotion. I decided anger can become a powerful motivator. An intense negative reaction to your circumstances revs up your internal motor more powerfully than a lightly held wish. I mistakenly told you these things.

Did anger help? No.

There was a point when your mind transferred your anger to your flaky boss, your overwhelming responsibilities at work; the crazy things drivers do; quirky things that made you scream at strangers; or that verbal crack you overheard and took offense at, or the slow waiter at our favorite restaurant. No one was immune to your anger. Not even me. We remembered the blame you tried to place earlier in your illness. You laughed when we talked about it. "At least," you said, "I had creatively come up with a new group to be angry with!"

You're dying. Is it any wonder communications become strained? The professionals talk about the 10 rules of engagement as a way to get through your anger (I can't even think of one now). For some, the method may work. Professionals, with their skills--and luck--can improve a patient's response to pain and lessen suffering and anger. There was a course that offered help. It was something to consider. And we did. We didn't take the course, but we talked about it.

There was something else I wanted to try. I had negotiated contracts when I was working. I thought I was pretty good at it. Let's see how good I am at negotiating with God. My earlier attempts at praying had not worked, but maybe things have changed enough that the channels are now open.

"God, if you'll just give us a few more years, I'll stop smoking and swearing. I'll even lose some weight. I'll exercise." I'm smart enough to accept that God probably doesn't bargain with those who already are in stage 4 cancer. But it's worth a try. "Can we bargain, God?"

I didn't hear a voice thundering down from the heavens with God's answer. In fact, I didn't hear anything. In my heart, a "few more years" meant 15 or 20 more. Maybe I was too greedy.

"OK, God. Was I asking for too much? You decide how many more years we can have together. Just tell me." I was trying to trick God by asking a question that I thought he'd have to answer with a number.

Looking up to the sky, I fully expected the clouds to part and a bright light to shine on me as God responded to my clever questioning in his Charlton Heston voice.

Who was I kidding?

Bargaining didn't work. I tried to get more time for my dying husband, but failed.

It took a little while for me to accept that my skills at negotiating with God were amateurish at best. The time came when I realized, as my partner had already done, that there's no give and take with God. I'd have to try something else.

Then I got depressed, really depressed. Again.

As the days passed, the pain you were experiencing grew worse. They have some great medicines that make the pain go away and replace it with sleep or stupor. When the pills or the injections were working, your life was only miserable. When the pain killers wore off, you writhed in pain. It was agonizing, watching you suffer. I wanted fast relief for you. Most of the time I couldn't get a nurse or a doctor to take care of you in what I thought was a timely fashion. But the doctors and nurses have other patients too. Sometimes you went through hell before relief came.

I suffered when you suffered, but it was not the same. I only experienced mental anguish. When your medication was losing its effectiveness, you multiplied your fears, trying to wrestle with your awareness that death was on its way, and with it, horrible physical pain.

Thank God for narcotics.

CHAPTER 5

DEPRESSED?
YES!

I THINK I understand how you must feel. I'm not sure, of course. I certainly tried to imagine what you were going through. I've lived with you and think I understand you. You didn't want to die; but you knew you were going to. I certainly could understand that.

But here's a question for which I have no answer: "How long does a dying person stay depressed?"

For you, the answer seemed to be that depression lasts until, reluctantly, acceptance pushes any thought of bargaining out the door. We had accepted the cold fact that death is inevitable. For you, depression preceded your acceptance that your time on this earth wouldn't be very much longer. It was time to start getting ready, to accept the inevitable.

Easy to say. I think that, for me, depression hangs around to the very end and then stays a long time after.

How sick does a man have to be when his "macho" frame of mind mellows, when he becomes tender to the needs of others, capable of a tear, a compassionate hug, or to become a listener who doesn't try to solve every problem?

How ill does a man have to be when his "I'll do it" personality drifts away, when he can graciously accept letting someone else do for him, to not feel obliged to do for others, to cry for no reason at all and not care who sees him, to take a compassionate hug from both women and men friends, or to become "just" a listener?

Depression takes over everything; all a person can do in this stage is feel sorry for himself. It's an overwhelming emotion.

You told me a time came when you decided that continuing to try for a cure or a way to put the cancer into a holding pattern took more effort than you possessed. You finally said to yourself, but not out loud, "I'd rather die."

I looked at you, wasting away day by day, trying to be lucid but not successful at it. Each day I waited as long as I could before asking, "How do you feel?" Then, after a short pause, continued with, "about things?" Then, there was the day you jolted me with your response.

"I'm going to die."

That was not what I wanted to hear. "What?"

"I'm going to die." There. I heard it again.

Was this a "depressed" person talking? I hadn't yet figured out what the "depressed" phase of dying meant. I had guessed it meant not talking much, sleeping a lot, being in a funky mood, and being pretty much down on everything. I didn't think depression preceded acceptance of being at death's door. You were acknowledging that Death was knocking, waiting for someone to say, "Come in." You answered, "Death, come on in."

We had been waiting for death to arrive; we were expecting the visit. It's hard enough thinking it; harder still hearing you say the words, "I'm going to die," out loud. Now, hearing you say the words that meant "open the door and let him in," made two of us seriously depressed.

I didn't know what to say. I gritted my teeth, took a deep breath, and said, "You've got to be kidding."

I wanted to hear you say, "Yeah, I was." I wanted to see that little upturn of your mouth you always got when you thought that something you said was exceedingly clever.

"I'm going to die." You said it again.

"Oh, oh, don't say that." I knew you had said the words we both knew were true. It was time to accept the reality that the doctors had been hinting at for the last couple of days.

Maybe it would be best for me to say, "You're right. I'm so sorry." Those words just wouldn't come out. In fact, my knees buckled and I had to hold on to keep from falling to the floor.

Instead, I moved beside your bed, standing, put my hands over yours and cried. Then I cried some more. After a few moments, we cried together.

How long would this terrible depression last? We were depressed because we knew your life would end. I felt terrible because you would be leaving me. That was a selfish thought. I was ashamed to let my feelings rise to the top of concerns. "I feel terrible," was the only thing I could say.

I started crying again. This time you tried to comfort me, but it took more physical strength than you had. You started crying again, too.

Your audible acceptance of your deepest fear was too much for you. After a while, you drifted off to sleep, exhausted. I stood there, my hands over yours. I tried, unsuccessfully, to think of something to take my mind off our terrible situation.

The thought of your body being in a casket, waiting to be put into the ground, was too much. "What can I do?" I said out loud to nobody in particular. Depression was an overpowering emotion. "No wonder so many people take pills to overcome it," I said to myself. "Can somebody give me something that will make this terrible, terrible feeling I have disappear?"

You groaned in your sleep. Then, stirring, you tried to pat my hand. The touch brought me back to reality with a start. There you were, barely able to take care of yourself, and you were trying to comfort me. "No wonder I love you," I said under my breath.

Just thinking about the difficult times that were ahead was a weight I could hardly bear. Then I realized that your thoughts were different. I imagined you could see the end and were wishing it would come sooner rather than later. You were probably saying to yourself, "When am I going to die? Why not now?" Then, stepping into the role of husband and father, asked, "What will happen to my family after I'm gone? Will they be able to get by? Will they have to get food stamps and stand in line for all the stuff they give to people who are in dire straits?"

I couldn't imagine anything good happening to me after your death. I could see you, though, fighting to stay alive a little longer so I wouldn't have to face that reality. Just the thought of how hard it was for you to handle your pain made me terribly sad.

"Come on, God. Do something.

"Is there anything we can do together that will help? Anything?"

It took the rest of that day and the night before I could guts up to accepting that your death was imminent. I didn't even try to go to sleep. I sat in the chair by the window and wallowed in self-pity. How could you die? Don't you know I can't let you die? I need you too much. I love you too much.

I spent the night sitting in that uncomfortable chair. Finally, about 8:30 on a morning I'll never forget, I shifted my position a little, squirmed a little, took a deep breath, and settled down again. I tried that little routine a couple more times before I was able to push myself out of the chair and stand beside you. "Good morning," I said.

You were already awake. "Sorry I laid that bad news on you yesterday," you said. Always considerate of my feelings, even when you're dying, were the words that ran through my head.

"It was quite a shock to hear you say it," was the best I could do.

"Yeah."

Was this a transitional moment?

Now is the time for one of us to be extremely brave. Who? You or me? You solved the question by saying, "I think we should do a little planning. Yeah...a little planning. You know...talk about what happens...after."

It was hard for you to say the words. You tried to look at me, but you couldn't. My knees felt weak. The words, "after," meant after death. A big lump was in my throat. I couldn't say anything.

"I did some of the planning when we took that 'Preparing for the End of Life' course at church," I said. At the time, I thought it would be several years before those plans would be put to an execution phase. "Let me find those papers; maybe they'll help us decide what has to be done." I choked on the words. How could we be so casual? My world was crumbling and yours was ending.

You nodded.

The train we were on was ready to cross the bridge. Is this what they mean by "acceptance?" Acceptance that death is a reality that's right around the corner?

What next?

"Will you do it?" he said. Those words were painfully said, and accompanied by physical pain. Clever as always, it was your habitual way to get the two of us to acknowledge in spoken words the inevitable. He wanted to hear me say "yes".

Asking if I would do something that acknowledged your coming death made me your partner in dying. I would be a participant in planning your final celebration, your "Going Away" party. The train was picking up speed. It took everything I had inside me to say, "OK."

I sat down. I looked at my shoes. I counted the tiles in the floor. I thought about the weather. I went through every excuse I could think of to keep from revisiting this conversation.

But I had to.

We had crossed the bridge and the bridge was tumbling down behind us. There was no going back. The two of us acknowledged that death was on the train with us. Now, to accommodate this new passenger, there were things to do. There were things to do, and I had to do them.

Well, there it was, just as the books say. I had tried to get God to give me more time. As a part of the bargain, I had offered him the only things I could, but I didn't hear him say, "Yes," so I figured the silence meant "No."

Depression was still tagging along. I discovered depression doesn't go away. It's a constant companion. No one can say, "depression, go away," and it magically disappears. I was depressed for months after your death. The mood elevating drugs helped, but a terrible feeling remained, bearing me down. It's a heavy, heavy feeling.

I guess, for me as a survivor, "acceptance" was the most difficult of the steps in the dying process. That's because I had fought and fought...fought until I couldn't fight any more.

I think everyone else had accepted the fact that you were going to die...soon. I still was hoping for a miracle. I had already been introduced to denial and anger; I knew them extremely well. I wasn't a good bargainer, so that step withered away. Depression hung over my head like the "Sword of Damocles," whatever that was.

You were going to die. You knew it. I knew it. This must be acceptance.

The two of us were going to talk about it as if we were talking about...what? The weather? No, we were going to get down and dirty. We were going to talk about you dying.

Oh, boy. What have I gotten myself into?

Did this conversation move ahead with me asking you a question and then writing down your answer? Did you alone talk and I put your words into "The Book?" Do we have someone else come and guide us through this preparation? Is there a list of questions I can buy and then the two of us answer?

Here it was again, that sickening feeling of dread. What have I gotten myself into?

After trial and error, we developed a little system that was reasonably workable. You would say what you wanted; I would write it down, with the understanding that, eventually, I would put everything into some order that made sense.

Right off, you started telling me the songs you wanted to have at your service. Next came descriptions of Bible passages. You couldn't name chapter and verse; that was my job. You remembered the story, or the point, or the event, and whispered that. I said, "You aren't making this easy for me, you know." I bit my tongue after I said it.

You smiled. "Sorry. This is the best I can do."

"Don't worry, I'll pull it all together," I said, grateful that I could recover from my earlier complaint.

Finishing this little project took several sessions, spread out over a month or so. After we got started, the hardest part was starting again. Who would say, "Time to work on your funeral?" Luckily for me, you were always the first one to bring it up.

CHAPTER 6

WATCHING YOU DIE

EVERYONE SEEMS TO fear death. To be more realistic, everyone wants to avoid the pain that precedes death. However, we race through life, running as fast as we can for the finish line that ends everything. Why do we do that?

How long had it been since this final part of the process had begun? A day? No, longer than that, even though it seems like just yesterday that this nightmare began. Months? How long had it been since you were able to have a meaningful conversation with family or friends? Too long. Everyone knew the end was in sight.

How long had it been since you had no pain? What started out as a little discomfort had now progressed to the point that even drugs didn't make the pain go away.

I hated it when you finally accepted the fact that you were dying; accepted that before long your life would end. How long would you be "you" before you died? We both knew death would be calling, but each of us had a different idea about when he'd knock on the door. I understood your idea of "how long" was not the same as mine. I knew it when you said, "too much to do; so little time."

It was pitiful. Previously so self-assured, so confident—all the traits that made you so successful—were gone. I looked at you. Your eyes were glazed, your arms black and blue from the many needles that had been stuck in your flesh, your hair unkempt, your face unshaven. This person lying in the bed was not the person I had known for so many years. You were not at all interested in what was going on around you.

The discomfort you felt towards the end was terrible. Your pain was so intense and hard to bear that increasingly large doses of opiates had to be used. When you started groaning and tossing and turning in your bed, the doctors knew you were very, very uncomfortable and the painkillers were wearing off. The doctors who specialize in pain management have so many different drugs they can use to achieve their objective of enabling their patients to have the best possible quality of life. Thank God. I think we tried all of them.

Looking back, the way the pain finally took over your every breathing moment makes me shudder; it must have been terrible for you. When your cancer was first diagnosed, you felt no pain; in fact, the major reason you doubted the diagnosis was because you felt no pain. But that changed over time. You did begin to feel pain, more each day. Now, even though you were drugged, you were groaning. The pain must be excruciating; your body was shutting down, faster and faster.

Suddenly, your eyes opened wide, and, in a whisper, you said, "I'm ready." As you said it, you sighed, as if the recognition and acceptance lifted an enormous burden off your shoulders. It had become more than you could stand. Your body was giving up and so were you. Your eyes closed.

I wasn't ready for you to die. Terrified, I said, "No, don't die. We need more time together."

But then I said the words I had never thought I could say, "It's OK. Just let go."

However, you weren't listening. Your lips moved; you had started a conversation with someone I couldn't see or hear. I couldn't understand your words, but I knew the person you were talking to could. I hoped the unseen person was giving you comfort modern science couldn't.

After a moment, you again opened your eyes, looking towards the ceiling. You tried to mouth the words, "I think I'll take a little nap," but it came out garbled, like "I trapnap." Then you closed your eyes again.

You slept almost all the time for the next three days. Occasionally, your eyes would open. You'd look around the room, mouth some words none of us could understand and then go back to sleep.

The hospice nurse told us to say our goodbyes because it didn't look like you'd make it through another night. She had been giving us regular updates on your condition.

You didn't die that night. You continued to wrestle with an unknown foe. You struggled, tossed and turned, and groaned. As a new day dawned, it was apparent death was wearing you down. I was exhausted, too. Late in the afternoon I succumbed to the wear and tear of trying to be with you all the time. I decided to take a little nap in that terrible chair I had spent so much time in. I had closed my eyes for just a few minutes but opened them with a start. What was it? Who was it? All I heard was your painful breathing. I was scared. But I drifted off to a fitful sleep.

Night came and I was awake. You were still waging that terrible fight with someone. An angel, maybe? I slept again.

Can you imagine the shock of awakening, looking at your partner and discovering he's dead?

We weren't sleeping together any more. Your illness made my weight in the bed something you didn't need. I slept either in a chair or on a small single bed, borrowed from friends. I was close by; close enough that many times in the night I would be able to hear you breathing, gasping for air, moaning because of pain. Sometimes I could hear you talking to ghosts or angels; I never could tell, nor could I understand your words.

A dead person is, well, dead looking. There's the paleness, the lack of color, no labored breathing. I knew you were dead the moment I looked at you.

My breath caught in my throat. I couldn't cry, couldn't scream, and couldn't call for help. I fell to my knees. When I tried to get up, I put my hands on your bed; my weight on the mattress made your body move. It was a surprise; I thought maybe I had been mistaken, that you hadn't actually died, and that when you felt the weight of my body, you turned to see me.

That wasn't what happened. As your body turned a little in the bed, a rush of air came from your lungs. I thought the sound of air escaping your body was your spirit leaving. I was terrified.

My mind raced through our conversations about what to do at your death. It was all written down somewhere. You and I had talked about "the day" you would die. Earlier in your illness, we had plenty of time to talk but we avoided any serious discussion as long as we dared. The pain wasn't so powerful early on; it wasn't controlling you yet, so we were reckless with the use of time.

You and I had no doubt about what would eventually happen. The doctors had made it perfectly clear that there would be no miracle cure. We knew that time was not on your side, that, as the destruction of your body continued, you would need pain killers (a bad, bad word!) most of the time and, as a result, be less and less able to think and talk. We were right.

You made the choice, finally, while you were still lucid, to talk about your eventual death. In my mind, those conversations were little make-believe games, not real. I guess I continued to look for a miracle to take away the cancer, even though we'd been told that wouldn't happen. That knowledge didn't keep me from praying we would get some special help from God. However, when you signed the directive that no heroic measures be taken to keep you alive, I knew you didn't expect any intervention.

I jerked back to reality. Still weak-kneed from my early morning discovery of your lifeless body, I stood beside the bed, looking at you. My mind cleared a little. Think! What's the plan? I went to the phone and called my brother. You and I had agreed that he would be the one to take charge; in fact, he had participated in several of our "discussions."

It was early enough in the morning that when he answered the phone, he knew why I was calling. I hardly got a word out of my mouth before he said, "I'll be right over."

When I hung up the phone, I knew a new chapter had begun.

It was OK for me to lose it; it was OK to acknowledge that my sweet husband was no longer in pain. It was OK to break down and sob. You were gone. Gone.

I lost it.

What happened next was so confusing I still can't sort it out. Friends came, neighbors came, pastors came, and family came. All tried, in their own way, to comfort me.

It's hard even now to say how many days I was zoned out. Other people did the necessary things. They later told me the plan you and I had worked out made their tasks easier.

The only thing that I can vividly remember was standing in our bedroom, getting dressed for your memorial service. You had been cremated.

CHAPTER 7

THE MEMORIAL SERVICE

IN THE PERIOD before your death, you had chosen to have a memorial service rather than a burial ceremony. You also chose to have the service in our church.

You didn't want the urn with your ashes to be displayed. We had previously discussed cremation or burial, without arriving at a decision. You made the choice in our planning sessions. You decided it was better to be cremated...and cheaper.

You always said you wanted a "different" kind of an end-of-it-all service. You talked about it enough, and I had made notes so we were able to make it happen the way you wanted. I don't yet know whether everybody thought it was a good idea or not, but the service was exactly what you planned.

There was a small jazz band stationed at the front of the sanctuary; they had played several songs before we came in, ones you had chosen. After the audience had been seated, the family came in. I was the last person to enter the sanctuary, holding on to someone's arm; whose I don't remember.

The audience stood up when the family came in. That was a very nice gesture, a show of respect. They sat down after I did.

The music continued. Have you ever heard a tenor sax, a bass, a piano and a drummer play "Amazing Grace" in a Dixieland format? Even thinking about it now makes chills run up and down my spine. It was so moving. Earlier, we had heard the combo playing while we were in the sitting room, outside the worship area. I'll never forget the sound of a tenor sax playing sad, sad music with a Dixieland beat. It seemed to me that the music set a tone of beautiful finality to your life

When "Grace" was finished, the band moved on to "How Great Thou Art." We were mesmerized.

As we sat there and listened to the music, I knew your preferences would make an impression on all of us that would provide conversational topics for years to come. I thought it was likely no one in the audience had ever been to a service where truly American songs were played. The soulful sounds created just the right atmosphere of remorse and respect. Then, surprisingly, the ensemble started playing "Jesus Loves Me." That lightened up the audience, and when they played "On the Sunny Side of the Street," some actually started tapping their feet. We didn't plan for the music to set the tone of the service so easily, but it did.

After that last tune, the minister got up. Uncharacteristically, he looked at the jazz ensemble and applauded. The audience joined in an unusual response from a very conservative congregation. I knew this feeling was what you wanted to happen.

The minister's opening remarks were brief and included a Bible verse or two which you had chosen. Not too much was said about you...yet. Then, instead of a hymn sung by all, or a solo, or music by the choir, the band played again. They combined three songs into a medley that continued to make your memorial service just that, memorable. They played without pausing, "Great Is Thy Faithfulness," "I Love to Tell the Story," and "Praise God from Whom All Blessings Flow." It was a musical tribute that expressed, probably better than anything anyone could have said about how you felt about living an exemplary life.

The minister read some more scripture, all of it in modern prose. You often said the Bible should be in the language of the people, not some stilted stuff nobody could understand.

There were no further words from the minister. Instead, several of your friends got up and recounted events from your life. We laughed and cried, then laughed and cried some more. When they finished, the minister said a short prayer, and it was over. Almost.

On cue, the band started playing again. There was no doubt about it; the music was the service. The statements by your friends and the ministrations to family helped. None would doubt that God was in that place. But it was the music we would remember.

The minister dismissed us, and as the crowd left, the band played snippets of "Softly and Tenderly," "There'll Be Some Changes Made," "In the Sweet Bye and Bye," and ended with "I'll Fly Away."

The "reception" was a sit-down meal in a rented hall, accompanied by appropriate liquids and more Dixieland music. It was a wonderful and joyous time, if you could say that about the celebration of the end of a person's life.

In the days after the service, I've become hyper—all the time.

My concentration has gone out the window (five minutes on any one subject—tops!). I can't carry on a conversation that involves thinking. I can't look anyone in one eye (let alone both eyes). I eat when no one's around; I must have already gained 100 pounds, and I'm working on the second 100. I can't sleep without taking a pill; however, some nights I drink instead of taking a pill (wine has proven to be an acceptable substitute for sleeping pills).

I've watched the bad stuff that's on TV late at night. After 1 a.m. or so, there are lots of sleep-inducing movies that no one would ever pay to see. I watch them.

In the morning after a particularly bad night (there were lots of them), I've asked myself, "Am I going crazy?" When I had the courage to answer my own question, I say, "Unless you get ahold of yourself, 'Yes.'"

Trying to come back to reality, I made lists of questions that required some mental agility to answer. Although the list changed every day as I made a little forward progress, I'm continuing to ask questions:

> Does grieving last forever?
> Why can't I figure out a way to handle this crisis?
> Will I ever get my life back?
> Is there any chance at all for normalcy?

One of the questions I should have asked required more courage than I had. I couldn't guts up to consider finances. I knew that day was coming, but I did my best to put off the day of reckoning.

There's this big, black hole in me, and I don't know what to do with it. Your death caused it. Most of the time, I'm unapproachable by anybody, content to be my own worst enemy. But every once in a while I start talking, uncontrollably. I'll talk to anyone. I tell them my deepest, darkest secrets. So far, I haven't been visited by any government agency, but I'm expecting them any day!

Late one afternoon, sitting in my favorite chair, feeling sorry for myself, and drinking a glass of my best cheap Chardonnay, I was trying to concentrate on the 6 o'clock news. At the same time, I was mentally continuing to bemoan my miserable state.

As I raised my glass to take a sip, I had an epiphany—a sudden intuitive leap of understanding—that started me on the healing road. It wasn't a miracle, but I'll never forget the words that formed in my mind. They were clearly understandable:

"You need help."

I almost fell out of my chair. This answer had been suggested repeatedly by my friends, to no avail. The need was now crystal clear, and I agreed. Where had this recognition and acceptance been before now? Probably right in front of me, but I was too foggy to see it, and probably too stubborn.

There was no doubt in my mind: I needed help. I think I had dug about as far down as I could go, and the hole was really deep. The only way left was up.

Help!

CHAPTER 8

REALITY — RIGHT NOW

I TRIED TO start the journey back with a little self-analysis.

Looking back at our wonderful years together, it's hard to believe the past is past. Our time together has ended—all that is left is memories. I hope you have terrific memories of a life well spent. I do.

After your death, I tried to look forward. I wanted to anticipate and plan for the not-so-distant future. I couldn't; I'd lost control. There was no way I or anyone else could guarantee the events of the future; no way to program life so that it would play out as I wished. Besides, even if I could, I wasn't thinking straight.

So I waited. And waited. Days passed.

One day, I sat myself down, intent on having a heart-to-heart talk with myself. I decided the reality of the present is closest to an event I could almost control. Good intentions are just what they say they are: intentions. But I'll try again. And again.

How long does "right now" last? For me, the present is much more real than the flawed remembrances of the past that had been my focus. Over time, remembrances gloss over the memories of unpleasant events and smooth out the little blemishes. I don't know how to get closer to anticipating the future than the very next second or minute. At best, we humans have only a little insight into the next few minutes of the next event.

It's only with luck that any domination is possible. No one I know can control the future.

I said to myself, "Don't waste it. Don't throw away this precious moment of reality because you think another time will be better. Whatever it is, do it now. This insight you're experiencing may be your path to recovery, your way back to reality." But what was "it"?

How can I savor the precious right now? So many competing events, thoughts, and physical needs make demands on my waking moments. The only way to take control that worked for me, which enabled me to choose from many options, was to decide what the most important thing was and do it. Ignore everything else and everybody.

What is important? Who knows? It was multiple choices. But I did it; I chose one out of the many.

After I had made a choice, my intent was to exclude everything else from consideration. It worked about 75% of the time. That meant I could start a task and, if I was extraordinarily lucky, complete it without distraction. I started by writing on a piece of paper things that needed to be done; then I would choose one item and start doing it.

That's a good approach, I concluded.

The hardest part was making the choice. But I'm getting better at it. Practice makes perfect. Reality was becoming attainable.

My companion is dead. How long has he been dead? I've lost track of the days.

What's next?

Historically, men die before their wives. As more women enter the work force, they feel the competitive stresses men feel plus the ones running a household creates. As a result, they're beginning to die earlier. I wonder if I'll have to work and keep house? I hope not.

I've read again some chapters in that book that were so helpful when my partner was in such pain. What would I have done without it? However, there's not a chapter in it that tells me what to do with the rest of my life. I looked through the book again for survivor instructions, but didn't find them. Unfortunately, I never got around to preparing my own book. That was a bad decision, but I can do it. But that still doesn't handle the issue of getting on with life.

It's 9 o'clock in the morning; family and relatives went home days ago, and my friends are not checking on me off and on all day long like they did for the first couple of weeks. I've read the newspaper two times since I got up at 6 (probably the earliest I've gotten out of bed in years). I've had four cups of coffee. I'm a bundle of nerves; jumpy from so much caffeine. What's worse, I've just about completed the crossword puzzle. And I said I wouldn't do them anymore. Sorry, God.

I've learned how the survivor process works. Right after the death of one-half of your life, you're smothered with attention and loving care. That lasts through the funeral or memorial service and then tapers off, a day at a time. There will be a day when you'll wake up, get dressed, eat breakfast, read the paper, and the phone won't ring or there'll be no knock on the door. Today may be one of those days. There'll be other milestones I'll recognize after they've happened.

So here I sit, head in my hands. This weekend our couple friends planned to get together for poker or bridge or barbeque, or whatever. Without a partner, I'm a fifth wheel. I should call someone and tell them I'm not coming. They'll object. They'll try to get me to come, but I know I'm solving a problem by not showing up.

I was depressed earlier, but now I'm really depressed.

I need new friends, single friends. I need new activities, things to do that will put me in contact with other lonely and grieving people. It could be the start of a new life for me.

I don't think I will ever remarry, I'm too old...and fat. Maybe I could at least have people as friends who are as unhappy as I am. I may need to join one of those groups like "Alcohol Anonymous." What do they call them?

I'm scared. It's a different kind of fear; it's fear of uncertainty. Oh yes, I was plenty frightened before. It didn't take my husband a long time to die, but I went through hell. I was the caregiver for the months he lay in bed. I admit it, I wore myself out. I'll never forget how I felt when I discovered my partner had died during the night: weak knees, serious vomiting, crying, wailing, and trying to roll up into an invisible ball. There's no way to describe how I felt. No one knows how terrified I was. Thank God the hospice nurse was there.

What I'm feeling now is a new kind of fear. It's a fear that requires response. I don't know a soul who can help me. I should be identifying a professional I can turn to or a support group. My mind races on from one unanswered question to another.

Am I going crazy? It seems I ask this question frequently. Should I call someone?

I never thought of this house as being big, but now I just rattle around in it. I think I'll move to a smaller place.

Hey, wait a minute. Now I know why they say, "Don't

make any major decisions until you've been alone at least a year." I will not make major decisions yet.

Confusion. Uncertainty. Doubt. I need to ask somebody for advice. Who? I haven't made an independent decision in years. I've always had somebody to talk with about the crucial things and to help decide. Now I'm the primary decision maker. Now it's life filled with uncertainties.

Money. Do I have enough? I'm working with the life insurance company now; how much will that bring in? Will I have to get a job? I certainly don't want to do something that will require me to stand on my feet all day. If I go to work, who'll take care of the dog?

The car. Oil changes, engine maintenance, tires. That car stuff is something I never had to worry about. You loved it. Maybe my eyesight isn't good enough to drive. On the other hand, if I don't drive, how will I get around? I can't depend on public transportation in this town.

My mind keeps listing issues that have been lying beneath the surface while you lay in bed, dying. There was a time when these were just topics to conjecture about; now with death and burial behind, the questions become the new reality. Every time I think of something else, doubts and fears rumble through my mind like an avalanche.

What will I do?

New tears. I've felt sorry for myself before and cried. These tears now are like nothing I've ever experienced. I'm scared to death. What do I call the anguish that has taken a hold of me? How will I respond to the emotional state I'm in now?

Call it "Survival Anxiety."

This is the new reality. It took a little while to arrive.

CHAPTER 9

SHIPS THAT PASS
IN THE VEGETABLE AISLE

A FRIEND OF mine had an experience different from mine when her husband died. His death was one of those long, slow happenings. Parkinson's is like that. It slowly creeps up on both of you.

Losing a companion changes things in lots of ways. For one, you suddenly have a new circle of friends—all with the same common denominator. When two survivors meet, there's an immediate bonding; a lost soul finding another lost soul. Your first thought when the new person you're talking to reveals that they, too, have recently lost their life partner, is "I can help this person." Then, if you're exceptionally lucky, you help one another.

I met my newest widowed friend in the vegetable aisle at our local supermarket. I thought I had met her before, so I spoke my best "Hello," to her when our carts collided. She gave me the "I don't know you; who are you?" look.

I told her I thought we had met at a grief-sharing meeting, but the pained expression on her face was not the response I expected.

"No," she said, and then, after a long pause, "I haven't gone to a support group yet."

"Oh."

She continued, "My husband has been dead eight months, and I'm still in the process of trying to pull my life together. So far, nothing has worked."

I just stood there, like a dummy, not knowing what to say. She solved the problem by extending her hand and saying, "Hi. I'm Ruth. I'm so glad you bumped into me." Then, conversationally, she asked, "How long has your husband been dead?" She had looked at the rings on my hand.

That question started our new friendship. We had other "in-common" things too. She had two dogs. I had a dog and a cat. She drove a late model Chevrolet; I drove a 10-year-old Ford. Her hobby was painting; mine was watching TV. However, our personalities clicked...and that's what mattered. We began meeting for coffee at the local Starbucks about once a week.

Today was the day she had decided to tell me about the journey that led to her husband's death.

She started with a short, unscientific, recounting of the way Parkinson's affected him. After telling me that although there are common characteristics of the disease, it affects each person in unique ways. She said, "We didn't recognize the warning signs until later. One day he said his foot felt like it was stiff and sorta dragging along. We didn't place any importance on his complaint; we both thought it would pass in a day or two. It didn't.

"The strange feeling continued. After a month, he started obsessing about it, and anxiety and stress crept in. His work wasn't yet affected. No one at his office seemed to notice anything, but he said the 'funny' feeling was driving him crazy. I don't remember how much time passed before a new complaint surfaced: he began experiencing muscle aches and pains that over-the-counter painkillers didn't help. One day a mild tremor ran through his whole body. That truly scared him.

"The tremors started occurring more often...and lasting longer. Then he became seriously constipated; this from a guy who had been as regular as clockwork with his bowel movements. I suggested that his concern over his physical health was causing it, and that explanation seemed to be acceptable. He did what we all do: he took a laxative."

"How long did it take for other symptoms to start appearing?" I asked. I knew a little about the disease, most of which I had picked up from TV. Parkinson's was first described in the 1800's by an English doctor named, of course, Parkinson.

She went on to say that over the next six months or so, other little clues started appearing. "We noticed that when he was tired or stressed, his tremors would pick up in intensity. When he moved about, they stopped. Well, they didn't actually stop; I should have said 'lessened.' At this point, the tremors were still not noticeable to someone who wasn't around all the time, but it seemed apparent to both of us they were getting worse. They were scary, and we began to think there was something happening that required expertise we didn't have. However, we didn't do anything, hoping against hope that whatever it was would just go away."

She continued, "I remember an event from years ago as vividly as if it happened yesterday. At dinner one night, he complained of difficulty swallowing; and I noticed he was drooling a little. He kept wiping his mouth with his napkin. I figured it was something in the food that was causing it.

"We made it through the rest of the evening. Later that night when we were in bed he told me he was seriously worried. I tried to take his mind off his concerns, playfully suggesting that spending a little time concentrating on my body might be just what the doctor ordered. It didn't work. In fact, right after my invitation he experienced a tremor in his legs. He jumped when it happened and that movement seemed to make the trembling go away. After that, he turned onto his side, away from me. I could hear him crying.

"The next morning he made an appointment with our primary-care doctor.

"The doctor's examination was short," she said. "During the course of looking and poking, the doctor asked him a question that got to me. He asked if anyone in his family had had Parkinson's?

"The shock of his inquiry was like being hit in the head with a hammer! Until that moment, I hadn't thought the problem was one that had a name. There was no Parkinson's in his family's history; as it worked out, he was the first. I learned from the doctor there's no cure for the disease, and the treatments they do have don't last forever.

"Here was a guy in the prime of life, ready for big time. He was 43."

She sighed. "In what seemed like rapid succession, other symptoms started. His balance was terrible. He walked in little jerking movements. Once he got started moving, he had a steady gait that didn't change. He only stopped when he ran into something or fell. Cuts and bruises became a part of our life. I noticed he stooped when he stood. He could no longer drive."

I started to ask a question, but she continued, "Needless to say, continuing to work was not possible; he took a medical leave which was followed by medical disability and early retirement. I remember this time of his life especially because his face often took on a mask-like appearance and he had difficulty talking. Later on his words were decidedly mixed up; he was often confused, and he had some wild hallucinations. His speech became increasingly hard to understand. His handwriting was illegible."

She took a deep breath, like you do when you've finished climbing a flight of stairs. "His physical and mental state continued to go downhill. The doctor told me to expect dementia, and he was right. He got to the place where he couldn't remember anything; when he needed a piece of information he couldn't dredge out of his brain, he started making things up. He had a great imagination. Where he got some of those ideas, I'll never know.

"Life was hell for him. Before Parkinson's, he was an uncommonly sociable guy who loved everything and everybody. Now his erratic movements and garbled speech were instant repellants, like opposing magnets. No one hung around too long.

"Though his ability to communicate was severely hampered, his mind was active most of the time. I can't imagine the thoughts he couldn't express.

"He tried to do things 'normal' people do. He would start out walking, pick up speed, and then stumble. He had only one gait: too fast. With increasing frequency, he had some serious falls. His arms were always bruised and black eyes and bumps were common."

She anticipated my question. "Oh, we tried all the treatments that were in vogue: surgery, medicines, and herbal remedies. Those events are a story in themselves. Someday I'll tell you about Parkinson's treatments and 'cures.' Some of the treatments helped a little while, but nothing made the Parkinson's go away.

"Life went on. Living with Parkinson's wasn't easy for me, and it was a nightmare for him. We went through all sorts of phases and stages. Together we grieved along the way for the loss of our lifestyle. When a couple deals with a long-term health challenge, it's like being joined at the hip; when one pulls, the other has to follow. Each of us had different emotional reactions. However, we both were affected by the pull. His Parkinson's ended up being a battle fought by two people, not one."

She finished her story. "One morning, 14 years after it started, he died. Looking back, it seems he had been ravished by Parkinson's forever. Nature had been so cruel, but his death was probably something he looked forward to, though I'm not sure. We never talked about it. I'm not able to describe adequately how much he suffered. I do miss him. My memories are of a healthy, smart guy. I try never to think of what that disease did to him.

"Now, I'm still trying to put myself back together." With that, she looked at me for understanding.

I couldn't help myself; tears were running down my face and I had to blow my nose. I couldn't say anything.

Loneliness is a common trait among us survivors.

CHAPTER 10

WHO FEARS DEATH?

EVERYONE FEARS DEATH.

Everyone seems to fear death. Or, perhaps more accurately, everyone seems to fear the pain that precedes death. I understand that now. I'm having second thoughts about things I was certain of months ago. For instance, being involved with the cancer death of a loved one is a lot different from listening to someone else describe their experiences. It's like someone telling you about their burn; it's different when you place your own hand on a hot stove.

I know the personal emotion of being touched by death. Realistically, I know that watching a loved one die is different from dying yourself. As an involved observer and someone who loved her husband, I've noticed a few things. Both of us were frightened, but in different ways. There were emotions involved for us, but they weren't the same. You were dying. I was watching you die and knowing my life would never be the same. You were reconciled to dying; I was terrified of living without you. I didn't want you to die alone, but I was scared of actually seeing you die.

Do those conflicting emotions make sense?

You once said to me, "Everyone seems to race through life, running as fast as they can for a finish line that ends everything. We want the finish line to be a long, long way away, even though we charge ahead like there's no tomorrow." I don't remember whether you were close to dying when you said that.

Getting old and looking towards the "finish line" is different from seeing the tape at the line before you're old. I know. Seeing the tape coming up fast is not a welcome indicator of a race you will be completing before you are ready. As life shaped the race, you were compelled to keep running whether you wanted to or not. You won the race in the prime of your life. That sucks.

Now, looking to a time after your death, I can say, "the past is past" with more than a hint of bitterness. It is not an easy transition from life to death. I remember saying to you early-on in your illness, "Oh, if only we were 10 years younger; maybe there's something we could have done to keep your cancer away. I know we'd do so many things differently." What things would we have done differently? I had no idea.

Before cancer, although we couldn't accurately anticipate events, we had a modicum of control. We learned we could not guarantee things will happen as we wished. Your illness was one thing neither of us anticipated. The guarantee period expired.

It's hard to face the reality of right now. But I have to. However, on the plus side, it's the present that I can come closest to controlling. I know the past is the past, and the future is, well, uncontrollable.

I don't need an essay on the use of my time. Not now. I just knew I didn't want to waste the precious moments you had left.

How could we have savored the weeks and months before your death? What more could I have done to make the moments before the end memorable for you...for me? There were so many competing events during the last period when death's march shoved everything else aside. I was saddened, confused, angry, and guilty—you name a dark emotion; I experienced it.

I focused on you and your needs and desperately tried to make the right decisions. Now, thoughts, physical needs, guilt, expenses—all are making demands on my waking moments. They are different demands from the pressures I experienced while you were dying, but they're all connected by you.

I know the advice I should follow, but it is advice I will not follow. I had previously gone through an exercise to decide what is important and should be done right now. It was a "do it" to the exclusion of everything else. While you were dying, I had no trouble prioritizing life. As your death came closer, making decisions was easy. There was only one: do whatever I could for you. Caregiving made relentless demands, but there was no competition. Your needs were always first.

I said out loud, to myself, "After all this time, there's no point in reliving your death, but I can't help it. I see something in the house that reminds me of you and the last few months come cascading back. When I dress in the morning and look at my jewelry, I see the pieces you gave me on special occasions and the last few months come rushing back again."

I remember when I asked God what was, at the time, the $64,000 question, "How long will my husband's suffering last?" He didn't tell me.

All the doctors could do was make a guess. I bet on months and years. I lost the guessing contest. Death won. Death frightened me. I don't think I'll ever be the same again. I know I won't.

After your death, a whole new life started for me. Widowhood is certainly a new experience, one I had not prepared for. It will take a while to make the emptiness go away. At this juncture, when I'll be able to enjoy a day is an unknown. It could be in a few weeks; maybe never.

People die every day. People die and leave loved ones behind. People die and the lives of those they left behind fall apart. There's no way to prepare for that emptiness even when you know it's coming.

What am I going to do now?

"This is just between the two of us, God." I was trying again to get some special help.

I've asked myself the very practical question, "What am I going to do?" a thousand times. When I couldn't answer the question, I turned to God.

Continuing, I said, "So far, you haven't given me a snappy answer." That definitive statement got the one-sided conversation going again.

I meandered on, whispering the words, "Here's the question one more time: I've lost the person that meant the most to me; we'll never be together again. What am I going to do?

"I've recognized healing is possible, and I think I'm getting a little better each day. You certainly are helping with that...thanks."

With a sigh, my monologue continued, "I reluctantly acknowledge that healing will take awhile. However, I need some big-time help recovering from my terrible loss, and I need some help getting on with my life.

"I understand my healing is irregular—some days are better than others—but it's ongoing. It's apparent to me healing will take a long, long time." I rubbed my eyes, trying to stop the tears that were forming, and continued my attempt at conversation, "Please God, please help me to have a life. I just want a regular old boring life, like everyone else.

"I'm trying to move away from focusing on the death of my partner. I'm trying to remember the good times we shared and the little things that made us happy. It's hard, but I think I'm gaining a little each day. I can plan, and that's a big step forward. I haven't yet made it to planning for several days ahead, but I'm gaining on the process. I now can take a positive action like making a reservation at a restaurant. That's progress, isn't it?"

I continued in the form of a complaint, "It has taken me so long to get to this point. I know it's different for everybody, but please help me heal a little faster. Starting a new life isn't an instant thing, and I know there will be setbacks. Can't you hurry things along a little?

"Thanks to my friends and You, I'm on my way to another chapter in my life. You are a part of the healing process, and I realize you may be making things happen at a different pace than I'd like. I know you want the very best for me.

"I'm looking forward to the day I'll be a new person, living with fond memories of an old life.

"Please help me."

With that plea for help, reality came rushing in. I can't yet answer the question, "What am I going to do now?" But there's a little crack in the black clouds. I can do some things now that I couldn't a month ago.

"Please help me," I asked again.

How do survivors survive? It's not easy, but they do.

I remember the first time I was alone in the house after the death of my partner. Family and friends had gone. There was no one to share a coffee with, no one to tell about my aches and pains. I was alone. Speaking to no one in particular, I said, "This is the way it will be...forever.

"Forever?"

Saying then the words out loud caused my stomach to turn over. I was sick at heart. I was terrified. I wondered how in the world I'd be able to go on? Would I ever again live a normal life, meaning a life like the one we had? I wanted the answer to be "Yes." I thought I was making some progress at surviving.

"Is there someone out there who would want to spend the rest of his life with me?

"I'm not interested in remarrying?" I asked the question out loud. It was not a statement, but a question. Boy, that was a sobering question.

Look at my body. It's not the body of a 20-year-old. It's familiar territory that has changed a lot over the years. There's a roll of "extra" here and there, a wrinkle where smooth skin used to be, a circle around the eyes, and without color, graying hair. I am the result of living with a companion who, over the years, added pounds, too. I have a body whose shape wasn't a priority item as the two of us shared a good bottle of wine or a high-calorie dessert. It's the result of naps, or the books I read when I should have been exercising, or the snacks before going to bed.

I then said to no one in particular, but trying to start a conversation with Mr. Reality, "I'm all alone. But it's not all over. It's not the end of the line. My life will continue on, even though right now I don't think that's possible."

Questions. At this stage it seems there are always unanswered questions. You've never balanced a checkbook? You've never shopped at a parts supply store? You've never bought tools at Home Depot? You've never changed the oil in the car? You've never made a Martini? Never chosen the wine at dinner? Never grilled a steak over charcoal?

Mr. Reality answered, "You're smart. You were smart enough to choose the best possible companion in the world. You were smart enough to get out of the way when it was time to replace a light bulb, repair an appliance that had jammed, or mow the lawn.

"You can get through this."

I can. Those words were becoming my mantra.

The family has returned to living their lives. Friends have returned to doing their own thing. Neighbors stopped bringing food a long time ago. I'm trying to get back to a normal life, but there's that nagging doubt, "I'm not sure I can do it."

Then, just after saying the doubting words, I mouthed the answer again, "I can get through this."

As a survivor, my life has been reformed. It's never been this way before, and I don't know how to handle it. My perspective has changed. What used to be done by my other half, or done as a pair, I now do myself or hire it done. Friends say my new single status will change my way of looking at facts. They're right. What used to get no thought at all because the other half of the partnership handled it, now becomes an item of primary importance that I have to learn to do (like putting together the income tax records!).

I've never worried about eating alone in a restaurant. I always had a companion to make conversation, to help decide what to order and to help eat the stuff that left with us in a "take out" box.

Your thoughts became spoken words, "I haven't even dented the surface of things that are different now. Everything is different. I can't imagine how I'm supposed to feel about the many things that have changed."

One morning you will wake up and things won't be the same. Not in a major way, just a little different. This almost-imperceptible difference is the beginning of healing. It's God's gift: the passage of time.

This new realization may happen as you sit at the kitchen table, reading the morning paper and having a second cup of coffee. It's no big thing. It's nothing more than the recognition that bad things do happen to good people. The death of your loved one was not your fault.

You need to get on with your life.

Recovery has begun.

Mourning, I discovered a critical fact: I can't rebuild my life by myself, I cannot recover without involving other people.

I had a bunch of folks waiting to help. All I had to do was ask. My friends were anxious to help, but I didn't let them in on my misery.

My family kept trying. They were the only ones that easily came to the house. They watched me in my miserable state, gathering in little groups and whispering things I couldn't hear but I imagined the worst.

I had access to doctors, both doctor friends and the ones you pay for; they took appointments and answered phone calls—if you made them. I hadn't.

Surely there were social workers and support groups available, but you had to initiate contact. I hadn't.

I knew about support groups—lots of my friends had been helped by cancer support groups. I intended to join my church's support group for persons who had lost a life partner. What do they call it? I hadn't checked yet.

I wasn't anxious to meet with friends, but I knew I should.

Trying to get my act together was tough. I kept doing the same dumb withdrawal thing repeatedly. It was hard for me to leave the house or make telephone calls. I blamed my hesitancy as being a part of the remorse process. It had to stop. "Surely," I said to myself, "I'm smarter than that. How many times do I have to make the same mistake before I learn it's wrong to keep sticking my hand into the fire?"

I remember someone defining insanity as doing the same thing over and over, expecting a different answer. That was me.

I could relate to a piece Portia Nelson wrote that described her life in five short chapters. I'm not sure my life is five chapters long, but it might be. Her story started when she, allegorically, was walking down the street and discovered a deep hole in the sidewalk. She fell in. Feeling lost and helpless, she didn't believe it was her fault. Getting out took a long, long time. I can relate to that.

Later, walking down the same street, she saw that the deep hole was still in the sidewalk. She saw it, but pretended she didn't. She fell in, again. It's hard to believe she was in the same place...again. She was. I am.

"Place the blame somewhere else," was her response. She still thought it was not her fault. Again, it took a long time to get out and resume life. I thought, "This is about the stage I'm in now."

Then, as she walked down the same street, she again saw the deep hole in the sidewalk. But she fell in anyway. Why? It's a habit. She did it with her eyes open. She knew where she was. She did it anyway. Getting out was still difficult. My take on that event was, "I guess that means we do things that are not helpful even when we know they're not."

Later, walking down the same street, she saw the deep hole in the sidewalk. She walked around it!

Still later, she walked down another street[1].

Where am I now? I'd like to think I was walking down a different street, not having to worry about pitfalls. I don't think I'm falling into any hole. I am a perfect example that it takes a while to get back to a normal life. I also believe that sometimes it takes several restarts before normalcy finally takes hold.

It was a question worth repeating, "How many times will I have to go into a funk and jump, willingly or unwillingly, into that symbolic hole? When will I be able to go another way?"

I accept that I need help...finally. Why didn't I recognize this sooner? I've said before that I need help, but apparently it didn't register. This time the awareness hit me like a load of bricks. It seemed to me that this recognition and acceptance represent a major breakthrough. I began beating myself up for being such a dummy and questioning whether I could do anything right.

Oh, how I wished you hadn't died.

Oh, how I wished you hadn't died.

When I'm alone in the bedroom with all the lights out, lying there in the dark, waiting for sleep, there are so many things to think about...and worry about.

I'm no spring chicken. In all likelihood, since I'm over 35, some would say I'm old.

I say to myself, "What are the things other people worry about as they age? Is there a standard list? Are worries different aging without a companion?

"Yes," I thought, as I answered my own question. Without a helpmate, a lover, a confidant—the special roles go on and on—life is different and difficult. A lot of things are different.

Is there any way to lessen the emotional impact that comes with the acceptance that death has caused some dramatic changes in my life—changes that can't be undone?

There are big changes yet to be made.

There it was again: the little voice inside my head.

Scary, isn't it?

My nighttime worries always start out the same, with a self-pitying litany: "I miss my partner. Life isn't the same anymore. There's this great big void inside me. Oh, how lonely I am."

As I lie there, there are other nagging fears bubbling to the surface. This is the part where I imagine terrible things. I knew the drill.

"Will I have a debilitating disease? Will I experience excruciating pain? Who will take care of me? Will my children die before I do?My siblings are beginning to show some of the troubling signs of aging. They're only a few years older. Is this what I have to look forward to?"

Then I enter the third phase.

I'm experiencing economic stress. I worry I'll run out of money before I die. Where do old people go when they're poor? If I need money, can my children help? They've got money problems of their own. I suspect they're planning on getting money from me after my death."

The questions continue, "Will I go to heaven or hell when I die? How about that problem my sister and I have had for years? Is there any way that dispute can be resolved?

"Who will take care of me? How will I handle the physical pain that dying may cause? Will I be awake as I die, or in a coma?"

The things to worry about continue multiplying about as fast as the minutes in the dark without sleep.

There are lots more things to worry about. My list isn't nearly complete.

I've convinced myself that I can make decisions, so I made one. I decided to give each major worry one day each week. I'll prioritize. On Mondays I'll worry about my kids. Tuesdays I'll worry about the number of pills I take. Wednesdays I'll worry about money. I'll fill out the remaining days in the week with major concerns."

This little bit of introspection ended when I said, out loud this time, "I've noticed there are always plenty of things to worry about. There probably are things to worry about I haven't even thought of...yet."

I remember hearing my father-in-law say, "Worrying must help. About 95% of the things I worry about never happen!" That was clever.

In spite of my best intentions and my new-found decision-making ability, there were emotional concerns that kept me staring at the ceiling in the dark. I grieved about my companion's death...again, about how my life will be different in the years ahead, and then, capping everything else, my inevitable death. Lists I had made became a low second priority when I thought about dying.

Back to thinking about the future: the fear of pain is always on my list of things to worry about. I just don't want to suffer a lot.

There are other nagging concerns, like "What if I've had a fall and banged my head, or my arthritis began acting up? I worry that I might have to have radiation for cancer, or maybe chemotherapy. Maybe both! Will I lose my hair?

How about balance? Even now, when I get up from a chair, I have to stand there for a minute to make sure my next step isn't the one that will put me face down on the floor.

It's easy for people to say, "It's time to get back to a normal life." Sure it is, although I'm not sure I can do it. Wait a minute: a normal life. What's that?

As you lay there, alone, in the dark, you say, "I won't cry. I won't." You're tough.

A tear runs down your face, and you stifle a sob.

Go to sleep.

Things are different now. No one can imagine how I feel or how things have changed for me. No one can. I'm miserable. A tear runs down my face, and I stifle a sob.

Go to sleep.

Things are different now. No one can imagine how I feel or how things have changed for me. No one can. I'm miserable.

I'm still trying to sleep, without luck. My mind rambles on: friends keep telling me things will get better. They are. But surely there's a way to speed the process up a little? I know my friends talk about me. I don't know what they say, but I don't like to be an object of pity.

I need to get to sleep.

Still thinking, I acknowledge something is beginning to change. What is it? When did it happen? I don't know if it began that night or at some other time. It just happened.

Was "it" an all-of-a-sudden event? No. Did it occur in a flash of inspiration? No. It is just slowly happening, a little each day.

I think—no, I am confident—better times are ahead. The time that's right around the corner will be the time I will be able to get in bed and go to sleep in a short while. I'll be able to go to sleep without thinking that in some way I was responsible for your death.

Guilt, real or imagined, is an albatross. If it would only fly away, I could go to sleep.

[1] *The story about repeatedly falling into a hole is from the book, There's a Hole in My Sidewalk, by Portia Nelson, Beyond Words Publishing, Hillsboro, OR. Copyright 1993*

CHAPTER 11

HOW MUCH GRIEVING IS ENOUGH?

"IF YOU ACT ENTHUSIASTIC, you'll be enthusiastic!"

I remember those words from my first job. The process works, sometimes. Right now I'm asking myself whether I can be enthusiastic even if I don't feel that way. The answer when I was much younger was, "Fake it and you can make it." I'm not having much luck faking it right now.

Maybe I haven't tried long enough. Malcolm Gladwell wrote in his book, 'Outliers', that true professionals—the really, really good ones—spent at least 10,000 hours working at their trade before they broke out from the rest of the pack[1]. As examples of people who were willing to pay the at-least-the 10,000 hour-price, he tells the stories of Bill Joy (famous for UNIX, a programming language), the Beatles (I know who they are!), and Bill Gates (the Microsoft guy)[1]. Spending 10,000 hours at a task, plus eating, sleeping, and taking care of personal needs... that's a lot of time, a lot of time, and a real commitment.

How long do I have to grieve before I'm expert at it? 10,000 hours is almost five years!

Here's a fair add-on question, "When I do become really, really good, can I quit grieving and do something else?"

Surely, I won't have to sit around and mope for five years?

Will I? Every book I've read, every therapist I've talked to, the ministers I've heard preach a sermon on grief, every friend I've shared with, every stranger who has heard my story: they all say that with time, grief can be overcome.

How much time?

It's hard to exactly pinpoint, but I remember the morning I woke up and things were a little different. Not in a major way, but just a little different. I guess that was the starting over point I was worrying about the other night. When do I cross the finish line? When can I say, "I'm a new, different person, ready to start a life without guilt? Without guilt because I accept that my life doesn't include my dead husband?"

How will I know?

OK, Sherlock...what's the answer?

There are books, small groups — opportunities all over the place that center on ways for singles to recover from their loss (call it "surviving"). It seems there's a television special every night about the problems of surviving. Psychologists and psychiatrists want to help, for a fee of course. And there are therapists and counselors.

It's a big market. There are so many types of singles: never-married singles, singles in crisis, divorced singles and survivor singles. The problems singles have support an industry. Just look for a book about single life in a Barnes and Noble bookstore; there are dozens.

Churches have taken on survivor's problems, too. Now, that's a missionary field that makes sense. It's especially true because there are so many different kinds of loss. Of them all, I believe the loss of a companion is the worst, even though loss of a long-held job is traumatic, too. Losing all your money in a stock scam fits in there, too.

Older adults have different problems from those in their thirties or forties. Age and financial issues seem to be great dividers. Younger people can get a job; those over 50 or 55 find it difficult to get work that pays minimum wage or, hopefully, more. Older adults don't seem to be the kind of worker fast food "joints" want to hire.

When I'm faced with a decision about what to do, what will I do?

Who can give me good advice, advice that's appropriate for my particular situation? Naturally, I don't want "general" information that's written for everyone. I want unique, very personal information. Where can I get it?

Sharing with another person who has gone through a similar experience seems to be a best choice. But that person may be so screwed up with their own recovery that they can't be of much help. What that means is I have to be very careful going through the process of grief and recovery. Pray for guidance, and pray that those you choose for help will truly be helpful.

I've got a lot on my plate; don't add more to it.

I've heard a sharing group is a great way to lighten the load of grief. I've looked into it before, but not seriously. I'd been told group membership gets you "survivor" support and, generally, a better understanding that the pain you're experiencing is not unique. That explanation proved to be true.

Changing lives for the better is what a grief support group is supposed to do. I could certainly stand a little of that. I don't know when a grieving person decides it's time to move on. If there's a test for it I haven't taken it yet. However, I've increasingly felt the need to have someone to talk with who might have an inkling of the emotions I was feeling. I decided to give it a try.

I started looking for support groups. A computer search turned up hundreds. I narrowed the list down to my geographical area and reduced the total number substantially. As my search continued, I learned there were lots of other places that list support groups that didn't make it to Google. I checked church web pages and bulletin announcements, the housing development newsletter, the local paper, civic clubs' web pages, neighborhood book clubs, the "Y," the Chamber of Commerce, University Women, and so forth. Apparently, there are enough people experiencing loss that it's pretty easy to get 10-15 persons to attend a first meeting. Whether they come back for the next meeting is the leader's challenge.

I ended up choosing a group that met in my subdivision, usually at the community clubhouse. I learned about it from the housing development newsletter.

I called the person listed in the newsletter. She gave me a little information about times, location, and stuff like that. But more important, she let me know there were lots of people like me that got together once a month on Sunday afternoons.

I showed up for the next meeting. There were about eleven of us. We all wrote our names on a name tag, but it didn't help much. Most of us couldn't read the letters without a magnifying glass. Surprisingly, there were more men than women. I sat down between two women about my age; one was fat, the other thin (skinny!). I thought to myself, "Maybe we look like those 'before and after' pictures you see in the diet ads." We introduced ourselves and settled in for the meeting.

The group leader was, as she told us, a retired school teacher. She had taught 25 years in the public schools, the last 10 as a guidance counselor for graduating seniors. Her credentials were as good as you could expect for "free." She fit right in with the group. We all were survivors, middle aged, middle class, and insecure. This was her second time guiding a group from the get-go, so at least she had reasonable expectations for us.

Her introductory remarks were qualifiers. She said the group was for people who had experienced the death of a partner. The group would be most helpful if the partner's death was caused by either illness or some traumatic event like a tragic accident. One guy, not trying to be funny, asked, "Does suicide count as a tragic event?" There were nervous chuckles, but no one said anything. The leader nodded; she then said, "Yes."

She introduced herself and then each person in the room told their name and a little personal information like the sub-division they lived in, whether they were still working or retired, nothing more. Things were a little strained as we attempted to assimilate the information that was being shared. Then our leader asked the "icebreaker" question: "Why did we decide to come to this particular group?"

She started the ball rolling by telling her own story. Her husband was killed in an industrial accident on an oil rig. If she had just stopped there, I would have been happy. She went on to describe the terrible fire, how her husband and three others sacrificed their lives so the rest of the crew could get off the rig. She then said her husband was a contract employee and the company who had hired him went broke, so there was no employer's insurance. He had no life insurance and what the government paid was not nearly enough. So, she went back to work.

Using her teacher's retirement income, she raised her children alone and helped them get through college. She now has breast cancer and will soon have to have surgery, chemo and radiation. Oh, the job she took after teaching was a cook at a fast food drive in. It paid just over minimum wage.

Her story made me (and I would guess, everyone else) feel like my problems were nothing. She had told us a short version of her story to help us get through our personal trauma—I felt like mine had just been swept over the bridge!

Another class member timidly raised their hand, looking around at all of us while waiting for acknowledgement from our leader. She got the nod, and started talking.

"I'm still having nightmares following the shooting of my husband by a robber who broke into our house...."

Her little speech got everyone talking. As we listened to one another's story, we realized our personal problems weren't the most terrible in the whole world. We were part of a group who needed reassurance and understanding. We needed each other.

This first session had been going on for about an hour when the leader said, "Time to break." We looked at her, stunned. How could this "thing" end? I felt more emotionally at peace since... when? How about since before my husband's diagnosis?

Subsequent meetings would have two parts: the first part would be the supposed-to-be non-stressful sharing experiences where we introduced ourselves to one another. Part two was a participatory exercise where everyone passed along the story of their personal trauma.

The leader announced the date and place of our next meeting and that, as a part of the meeting, she had asked a professional grief counselor to tell us about her work.

I hadn't told my story; we ran out of time. I had planned to talk about the part where I burned out, how my physical health suffered, how my friendships evaporated, and all my other problems. I had thought my story would capture the sympathy of the group; now I knew there were others who had suffered as much or more than I. A partner's illness, death, and the remaining partner's survival issues were common themes. As I listened to their stories, the similarity to my own was remarkable.

I had expected to hear some emotional narratives. I did. I had expected the atmosphere in the room to change as we shared one another's pain. It did. We all acknowledged our personal experiences had a dramatic impact on our lives and that we all had memories, difficulties, pain, and, fortunately, some remembrances of laughter and joy. I didn't think any of us experienced a miracle of healing and character change in that first meeting. I didn't gain a profound depth of insight into my own issues, but I had hope that several meetings like this might cause it.

In this first meeting, although many spoke of their love for their dead companion, no one had wondered out loud if they would ever find love again. I suspect that question is lurking in everyone's mind.

However, there was an outflow of caring and our little group began to bond. Everyone seemed to want to help the others. It's safe to say that in that first meeting we all experienced, at one time or another, warmth, laughter, and tears.

As we stood around after the meeting's end, eating and

drinking, more than one person said how grateful they were for a forum where they can ask for help from others who understand their situation. The dynamics of the meeting were remarkable. Regardless of our working and social backgrounds, strangers became "best of friends."

It only got better and better with each subsequent meeting. Our little group stayed together for 10 sessions. We developed the routine that, after each of our meetings, we went together to a restaurant, or a bar, or someone's house where our fellowship continued.

This addition to my life created a small light at the end of the tunnel.

[1] *Outliers, Gladwell, Malcomb. Published by Little, Brown and Company, New York., 2008,*

CHAPTER 12

MY OLD FRIENDS
DON'T FIT ANY MORE

I NEED SOME new friends. I don't fit with my old ones. They're couples. I'm not.

Everyone says, "Join a singles group." They didn't mean the survivors' group I was going to. They meant a singles group whose members were ready for action!

I tried that. Everyone there was either on the make or they're fat. Or ugly. Or narcissistic. Or depressed.

There's something about a singles group that didn't appeal to me.

Someone else said, "Try going to the singles bars."

I tried that, too. It seemed everyone there was trying to make a liaison that ended with sex. A lot of them were fat. Or ugly. Or narcissistic. Or depressed. The bars were a repeat of my earlier experiences with single groups.

I'm not ready for singles groups or bars as a way to make new friends. The survivors' support group is helping, but that group has problems similar to my own.

Over time, I've tried just about every suggestion anyone has made to me. Right now, the best thing I can think of is to go to my Singles Sunday School class. I'll go to it and sit and wait. There may be some hope; it's a large group, and there are several singles just like me in the class.

If the church class doesn't work I think I'll run an advertisement in the paper.

Just kidding.

I had decided to try to get a social life again. Unfortunately, I didn't know how. In retrospect, luckily for me, the opportunity presented itself without me having to initiate anything.

My friends (the couple friends we socialized with when we were a "pair") had previously called to invite me to join them and others in a social event of some sort. Sometimes it was Bridge; sometimes it was dinner at a special restaurant; sometimes it was cocktails and dessert.

When my husband was alive, these get togethers had been something the two of us looked forward to. We took our turn, too. Every once in a while we would host the gang for an event. Our specialty seemed to be the theater. Our little community had a very active amateur theatrical group, and they put on several plays a year. It was always great fun. We'd meet at our house, have a drink and then go together to the theater. After the show, we'd go back to our place for dessert and coffee. We loved it.

Since I had become a "widow" (a term I was beginning to use more and more often), I hadn't been to anyone's house, or any other social gathering, and I sure hadn't had one on my own.

The call came late one rainy afternoon; one of those days when it's easy to be despondent and depressed. I needed something to cheer me up, and the invitation was just what the doctor ordered. The gang had decided to meet for cocktails, dessert, and coffee. Nothing fancy; just a chance to catch up on the local gossip and revitalize friendships.

I accepted.

After I had hung up the phone, the worrying started.

What would I say when someone told me how sorry they were that my husband died? What would I say when they asked me what I was doing these days? Had I decided to go to work? Was I playing a lot of Bridge or Mah Jongg? How was my car running? Who is doing the little repair jobs around the house? Someone would surely find a way to ask me if I was interested in meeting someone?

What would I wear? Was I still in widow-garb? Deciding what to wear has always been a 20-questions routine. I would pick one outfit, hold it in front of me and look in the mirror. I wouldn't care if the first outfit looked like a million dollars, I still needed to keep up the routine of "hold it front of me and look in the mirror as many times as I had possible outfit options."

I still had a couple of days, so there was no need to panic...yet. I walked into my dressing closet and saw, for the first time in many months, "dressy" clothes. I stared at the suits and cocktail dresses. Did these really belong to me? They looked like they were made for a woman who easily wore size 6, or maybe an 8. I just knew I was a size 98 now. A big tent was what I needed. Grieving, for me at least, meant consuming lots of "comfort" foods like ice cream and pie and cake and martinis and margaritas and wine and other gobbledygook with lots of calories.

I pulled from the rack a little number that looked like something that might fit. Dare I try it on?

I stepped out of the clothes I was wearing, closed my eyes and slid the dress on over my head. When I felt it rest upon my shoulders, I shivered a little. That body tremor caused the dress to settle a little more. My eyes were still closed. Gingerly, I peeked out. Nothing yet. I walked over to the dressing mirror and stared at the person in the mirror. It was me! The dress was tight, yes, but I had gotten into it. If I didn't breathe, this little number might work. My prior habit of checking several outfits before I made a decision went out the window! Take what you got and run with it! It was an easy choice. I did.

Quick, get out of it before it rips.

I put on my grungy jeans, hung up the dress and proceeded to pour myself a congratulatory glass of wine.

The get-together night arrived. I don't think I'd eaten anything from the invitational call until I took a bite of an egg roll in my neighbor's living room. My fast was not brought on by a desire to lose weight; it was nerves. Everyone stood around like the ice in the pond would break at any moment. Here I was, drink in hand, doing my best to play a role I had never played before. My friends knew, of course, and they were trying to make it easier for me. Everyone was there, probably because they wanted to see how I would perform at my first outing without my husband.

"Yes, thanks," was the answer to the most asked question of the night, "Are you OK?" No one had the courage to ask if living as a widow was hard. They knew the answer to that query. They could look at me, changed a lot from the last time we were together at the Memorial Service. I was thinner than they'd ever seen me (even though I knew I was fat, fat!). They knew the pounds didn't come off because of some wonderful new diet. But, from an appearance perspective, I must have looked pretty good. None of my friends could say they now weighed what they weighed when they got married. I could.

We all made it through the evening. I did better than I thought I would. I didn't cry, I didn't spill anything on my dress, no one patted me on the shoulder or said, "Things will get better after a while."

When I got home, after I closed the front door, kicked off my shoes, I couldn't help myself; I heaved a big, big sigh, and then started uncontrollably crying.

When, at last, I got over my crying jag, I tried to review the events of the night. It wasn't pretty, but it wasn't too bad.

But a hurdle had been overcome. I might never be asked to another couples party, but at least we all made it through the evening. If they voted my continued participation in or out, I'm pretty sure I'd be out.

I could imagine my friends talking about me. They were probably saying things like, "I don't know how she does it," and "Isn't she brave." I could also imagine them saying, "I tried to talk with her, but we couldn't find anything in common. She's so different."

How does a recent widow get along with her married friends? Everybody is accustomed to speaking, "We did this," or "we did that." They don't know the questions that have to be answered when you're one, not two. I did. I also knew there were questions I'd be answering long before I was ready.

Oh, why did you die....

CHAPTER 13

A PERFECT MOMENT

I REALLY NEEDED help getting my life started again. I'd come to that conclusion several times, but hadn't yet figured out how to do it. I'd reached the point where I openly admitted it. I'd read books and talked with lots of people, and, of course, prayed about it.

I've finally started a routine that has a good possibility of being an important addition to the recovery puzzle. I got the idea from a book about a dying man who chose to make a list of people who had influenced him and to contact them before he died. The book is "Chasing Daylight," by Eugene O'Kelly.

It started with deciding when the time was right to get started. I waited for inspiration of some kind, and I got it. To this day, I don't know how, it just happened. From time to time, when I felt I was ready and the mood was right, I stopped. Whatever I was doing, I stopped doing it. This mood could hit anytime, but most often in the early afternoon. Sometimes the "right" time happened right after my evening meal. It also randomly occurred. I eventually concluded that when it happens is not important, but to just go with it when it does.

I sit down in a chair by a table I can write on. I think about the people I've known, those I admire, love, or just remember. The list was not put together on a selective basis (I'd save that for later), I just added the names as they came to me. When I thought of someone, to make sure I didn't forget, I write their name down—I'm making my list in a spiral notebook. The list is the kind I'll add names to from time to time. I keep the list handy, always in sight on a table or chair. You know how it is: sometimes names pop into your head at the craziest time!

There's nothing sophisticated about the process. When I think of a name, I write it down—after all, it is my list. I learned the hard way to write the name down the moment it popped into my head. If I didn't, the name would go back into an unapproachable spot in my head.

The names I've come up with include family, relatives, church friends, neighbors, associates from clubs and civic organizations, colleagues from work and classmates from grade school on. I never know where another name will come from; it just shows up in my head. I'm told the average person knows about 200 people. I'm not there yet with my list, and probably will not even get close. The names represent my circle of friends; perhaps it's what they call "my circle of influence," whatever that means. The names are the people who've helped make me the person I am today.

Creating the list is taking a lot longer than I originally thought it would. When I decided to do it, I thought it would take a couple of days. A couple of weeks have passed and I'm still able to think of a name or two every day.

Some of the persons are grade school friends I haven't contacted since the sixth grade. Some others are business friends who no longer are in business. Of course, there are neighbors and church friends. Some of the names I recalled really surprised me; at the time their name came into my head recollecting what we did was not particularly something I would want to remember. But I put their name in the book anyhow.

After I'd been working on the list about a month, I began

my first serious review. I wanted to try out my idea even though the list wasn't yet complete. I sat down at the kitchen table—it's warm and quiet there, a comfortable place. I got a cup of coffee and just sat for a few minutes. It was an "enjoy the moment" moment.

I took the list in my hands. Starting with the first name, using my initial notes as a starting point, I tried to recall in detail where and how we met or the special thing we did together. I wrote what I remembered. Then, I moved forward through the years and recalled other specific good times we'd had together. I said to myself, "Why did I think of this person? Was he/she a close friend or just an acquaintance? Do they have a talent, a trait, or a quality I've always appreciated? Have they been extremely helpful to me in a situation?" I reflect on how I'm undoubtedly a better person because of knowing them. I write some more notes that will help me recall my thoughts at another time.

Each person has their own page (or pages) in my notebook. I want to remember everything that happened, starting with my original notes, so I've written my recollections in a notebook to make sure they don't get lost. Each person has his or her own page (or pages), sort of like a chapter in a book.

After a while, I learned that whenever I was having a difficult time working with the list, to stop and do something else. As my list got longer, I decided to break my reflective time down into manageable chunks of two or three names. That was smart.

Next was what I considered the second step in the process. I was still adding names to my list, but I wanted to get a "feel" for what I was doing. I congratulated myself; that was a smart decision. I actually reached around to my back and patted my shoulders a couple of times!

The second step was making contact. Finding the city they lived in, then getting their address or phone number, was not easy. Luckily, some of the contact information I had in my files; the other names took research and that takes a lot of time. Some of them are dead. Finding that out was a bummer.

The computer was wonderful; it made searches in seconds that would have taken hours (or days) to do with manual research. However, adding details to the list was a major activity and took an awfully lot of time.

Once I had contact information, I had choices: if they lived in my town, I could physically go to their home, I could call, or I could write. Of course, the first alternative of actually seeing them face-to-face was not possible for those who lived somewhere else.

My objective, regardless of how I connected, was to tell them explicitly the memory event that brought their name to my mind. Then I would tell them how I feel about them. I had decided every discussion would be about good things; no "get even" contacts.

The easiest task was making contact face-to-face. Next was on the telephone. Talking on the phone turned out to be what I did the most, because many of them had moved on...their careers took them all over the world.

Starting the conversation (after the "Hello's," "How are you?" and "It's been a while since we've talked") is where it got hard; after all, where had I been in the intervening years? And in some instances, why had I waited so long to make contact? Luckily, not one person said, "Who are you?"

I settled on a little opening script for both face to face and telephone contacts. It went like this: "Since my husband died, I've spent a great deal of time thinking about events of the past. Your name kept coming up in my thoughts." Then I tell them some of the stories I remember about the two of us, or some other memory we both can share. Then, the clincher: "You were a great influence on me, you know. I just thought it was time for me to tell you how much I appreciate you."

I pause. They'll say something, and we're off and running.

I try never to forget why I'm making this contact: it's my way of saying, "You helped me grow up," or "I'll never forget the time we," or "You enabled me to change," or just, "I really appreciate you," or, "I love you because...."

This little exercise has been really good for me. I discovered, in addition to relating what they've done for me, in many instances I had touched their lives, too. I've had tears on my face many times since I started this project. Hearing about the major events in my friends' lives has helped me get a little perspective in my own.

I'm sorry this idea came up after my husband died; it would have been fun to do it together. This exercise for survivors (as I subsequently named it) was interesting. It was, I decided later, the preface to a perfect moment.

How flattered would you be if a friend called you out of the blue and began sharing memories of life-changing events from the past that had involved the two of you? Conversations like these are the making of legends.

The visits with the people on my list naturally involved events from the past. (That makes sense!) I also discovered it was not likely the two of us had ever before had a conversation like the one I initiated. As we talked, we both had an opportunity to create something special, a new memory, and a perfect moment.

I call a "perfect moment" a little gift of a moment or an hour or an afternoon with a special person. It's not a temporary thing; this moment in time will stay with me the rest of my days. I never know when the "moment" is going to happen, or with whom it will be. It doesn't happen with every person I talk with. I wish it would happen frequently. As I've said, the time we spend together can be face to face (the best), on the phone, or in a letter (letters are the most difficult because it's a one-way conversation).

Time really can't stand still, of course, although there are the perfect moments when it seems to. I know of no easy way to describe this kind of a very special event, this perfect moment. I knew it was extraordinary as it began to happen. Before I started contacting the names on my list, I couldn't make a perfect moment even if I wanted to—I didn't even have an idea of what a perfect moment was. But as the project unfolded and I became more confident, I was able to set aside the time and create the atmosphere where a perfect moment could happen.

In a perfect moment there is a little gift. The gift is always a surprise. In order to enjoy it, all I had to do was be open to the moment. After a while, I learned not to get frustrated if it didn't happen. I keep trying.

Here's how it works: as the two of us talk, I try to focus on a special event or conversation that pleased both of us and brought back a pleasant memory. When both of us remember, sometimes I laugh out loud. Or sometimes I cry.

As I describe to my friend the event we were talking about, I try to get a picture of it in my mind. When it was hard to make memories come alive, I would keep talking about anything, sports, news, movies, plays—anything. I was trying to experience time in a special way. I was seeing a vision—some thing that brought me joy or serenity. It could be as simple as a memory of sitting on the front porch of my childhood home with my friend, or a funny event that happened to us when we were in high school. Or, it could be something crazy that a bunch of us did.

Can you imagine talking with a friend and revisiting the good times you've had in the past? If that friend is one you haven't been with or seen in quite a long time, the conversation will be remarkable. You're given the opportunity to relive a special event from the past. When it actually happened you probably didn't have the perspective on life to place a lot of importance on it. Getting older helps bring events into focus. The remembrance comes together in a way that is unique, to be treasured. It's a perfect moment.

A perfect moment is what it is. There were no fireworks or spectacular happening, or an amazing revelation of any kind. It was just a perfect moment. I knew it when it happened.

The more perfect moments I experienced with my friends, the easier it was to create another perfect moment.

When I couldn't do it I didn't worry about it. When it happened, it happened. When it does, it's as if Angels have visited.

A lot of things have happened since I started this project. My life continues to be more complicated and I don't spend nearly enough time contacting old friends as I should. But I still do it. I've filled several spiral notebooks with notes.

A big plus is that some of us are now in regular contact with one another.

CHAPTER 14

IS THIS WHAT IT'S LIKE TO DIE?

OH! I OPENED my eyes. All I could see was the glow from the night light in the bathroom.

There it was again. This is why I'm awake. The pain I felt was like being struck by a bolt of lightning or being hit by a large truck.

Oh! There it was again. I could feel a fire burning in my stomach. The only way to put it out was to get rid of it.

I jumped out of bed—probably broke the world record for that task—and headed towards the bathroom.

'Didn't make it. I upchucked right in the middle of the floor, on the carpet. It was an involuntary spasm that nature made me make. It was embarrassing, but I had no control over it. It happened sooo fast.

I didn't even have time to feel sorry for myself or to be thankful there was no one around to see what I did. Unexpectedly, nature made another emphatic statement to me. I hurried towards the stool, sat on it, and had another involuntary eruption. I can't describe exactly what happened, but I also doubt I'll ever forget it.

Then it was over. Wow!

Whatever it was that was inside me is now out—on the bedroom floor and in the sewer.

The pain that I had experienced a few minutes earlier was now gone, too. It was almost as if it had never happened, except I had a mess to clean up.

Standing at the sink, I washed my hands and splashed cool water on my face. Talking to myself, I said, "I guess I'd better clean that mess off the floor. If I wait until morning, it will be a lot worse than it is now."

I turned on the bedroom overhead lights, peeked down at the mess, and then proceeded to go to the kitchen to get the necessary cleaning supplies. "I wonder if I'll have to have the professionals here to finish the job?" I asked myself.

By 4 o'clock the next afternoon, everything was back the way it was. The rug cleaners finished up my amateurish job, and everything is now as good as new.

I'd been so busy I hadn't had time to reflect on what had happened. Sitting in the family room TV chair, I reviewed the events of the last couple of days. "It had to be food poisoning; nothing else would have caused me to react that quickly," I said to myself in my most detective-sounding inner voice. "Last night's meal was delicious, but it also really packed a wallop!"

"Oh well, onward and upwards," I said. Suddenly, I stopped. That was what you said whenever we had to clean up a mess. I hadn't thought of that phrase for I don't know how long. Memories of our past life came flooding in. I cried.

After a little bit, I got my act together again. Leaning back in the chair and putting my feet onto the recliner stool, I tried to get some perspective on what had happened to me less than 24 hours ago.

"What if I had been really sick, couldn't get out of bed and couldn't reach the phone? Who would ever know? I could be dead for days before anyone checked on me."

The first thought that came into my head was to get one those things that you wear around your neck. In a situation, you push the button and someone is supposed to respond. "What if I can't talk? What if I've had a stroke and couldn't use my hands?"

Then I remembered reading about women who call one another each day at a specific time. If the person being called doesn't respond, the caller calls 911. That sounded like a good idea. If I'm lying in a pool of blood, just about dead, 911 will be here right after I get my friend's call and don't answer the phone.

The only problem: what if whatever terrible thing happens to me right after I've talked to my phone mate? It'd be 24 hours before I got checked on again.

The button necklace sounds better and better. How about both?

I didn't solve that problem. Like so many important issues, I put it on the back burner and played Scarlet O'Hara by deciding I'd resolve the problem later.

"Hope I'm not sorry."

Why is it so easy to remember the bad things from over the years? Why don't the good memories come easier? Perfect moments are hard to come by.

I don't know the answer to that question. It bugs me that it's a true statement. I think it was when I started contacting old friends that the question first came up. I noticed that when I was trying to go to sleep (or sometimes in the afternoon when I'm having a cup of coffee all by myself), troubling thoughts race through my mind.

I had spent a lot of time reliving good times with old friends; why should the process change and I start remembering negatives? I hated it when this darkness started.

I remember the things I did as a youngster that got me in trouble. I remember a lot of the things I did no one ever found out about.

But I remember them. These are the things that happened over the years—bad things—that come racing into my mind.

Go ahead, feel sorry for yourself. It doesn't do any good to know that lots of people have the same guilty conscious problem. What are you going to do about your bad memories?

It wouldn't do any good to recount that stuff out loud. Even if I were a Catholic and told the Priest in confession, so much time has passed that nothing good would come from the confession. Oh, I might feel better, but I doubt it.

I can remember every argument you and I had through our marriage. I can remember how I hurt your feelings and how long it took me to make up to you. Why can't I have the same vivid recall of the great sex we had? We did have some great sex, too. Just thinking about it right now brings a smile to my face...and other things to my body. Unfortunately, that's not the thought that most often springs into my brain. Luckily for me, those passionate memories do come back.

This easy remembrance of bad things is an imponderable for me. I wish those bad memories would go away.

Here's how it works: I remember the time in the first grade when Ms Davis looked at my attempt to print some sentences on a page. For some reason, I was printing the sentence backwards. The sentence was something like, "See Jane go up the hill." I had written, "hill the up go Jane See." (I later learned about "palindromes," which is a word, sentence or phrase that reads the same backwards or forwards. I was not doing that!)

It took a little while for her to straighten me out, but, good for me, she did. Why did I even remember that episode? This little story is tame compared to some of the stuff I recalled!

Lately, there are lots of reminiscing events like that. In retrospect, those bad or crazy occasions must have had a serious impact on my memories. I say that because the memories keep coming back. Why can't I remember winning the sixth grade essay contest, or my starring role in the junior high play, "Bertha, the Beautiful Typewriter Girl?" Or the first time I was kissed? (Honestly, I do remember that!)

Maybe it's your fault. Can I point to the time I started remembering the bad stuff was when you could no longer get around without help? Or maybe it started when you groaned with pain? Maybe it started when you told me you were going to die soon?

Bummer.

Acknowledging the bad stuff that filled up my head hasn't helped. Nothing I've done so far has kept the bad things I've done from popping into my head, uninvited. For instance, last night, out of the blue, I started remembering a time in high school when a group of my friends went into Woolworths' Variety. Our objective was to shoplift a piece of jewelry. We thought it would be exciting to live on the dark side for a few moments. We stood at the jewelry counter, waiting for the "right" opportunity. We all did our stealing thing (with a lot of nervous fumbling) at the same time, hiding the costume pieces in our clothing. We then proceeded to leave the store and walk down Main Street, giddy with excitement.

All of a sudden, a man appeared right in front of us. We were "nabbed." Embarrassed, we were marched back into the store and into his office. It took a lot of crying to keep him from calling our parents. Needless to say, we were cured of any desire to shoplift. We left the store, heads down and shuffling along, hoping no one we knew would see us.

Why did that memory come back? Was I being punished?

Was it guilt because I had not lived the kind of life that would have kept you from getting cancer? That was the troubling thought.

Of course my past didn't cause you to get cancer or to die. Or, did it?

The more I thought about it, and I thought about it a lot, the more I became convinced there was a message for me in everything I was remembering. I eventually put a very positive spin on my memory trips. Some of the things I had done in the past were unpleasant, humiliating, and sometimes the result of bad luck or lack of preparation. Bad as they were, at the time each happened, I learned from the experience and gained insight that helped me as I grew older. I now am able to handle the "downers" that occur fairly well. With each lesson, I became a better person.

In a sense, your death was a mental catharsis for me, bringing to the surface repressed emotions, complexes, and feelings. Believe it or not, your suffering helped me identify and end the guilt I felt. You started moving me along the path to become a better person, a mentally healthy person. Wow!

This gestalt jerked me back to reality, back to a survivor mentality. I was able to concentrate on our lives together and the good times we had. The bad clouds faded into the sunset.

Let's have a party!

CHAPTER 15

GETTING ON

GETTING ON WITH my life doesn't mean forgetting you. Wherever I am, whatever I am doing, whoever I am with, I can celebrate my old life. I can now do it without falling apart, or feeling guilty.

Why don't I do something that will be a memorial to our life together? Something like:

> Plant a tree
> Make a donation in your name to a favorite charity
> Set up a scholarship fund (If I did something like this, I could ask others to contribute; that way greater good can be accomplished.)
> Have a memorial golf tournament
> Do something very personal for myself each year on the anniversary of your death
> Throw an anniversary party

I decided that doing any of these things, plus the passage of time and the development of new interests, would enable my grief to fade, or at least become controllable. I was partially right.

There was always the nagging thought, "How long will it take for the past to really be past? How long will I grieve before I can start a new life?" The answer was right in front of me. I didn't realize it at the time, but the answer was it would take longer than I thought.

The restoration to living a normal life doesn't happen on a schedule that can be controlled. It takes as long as it takes. Day by day, I re-entered the world a little further. I had a long way to go, but I was making progress.

Here's something else I did: talk to my companion's spirit. You know, have a conversation. I did. Occasionally I would bring him up-to-date on my life. Not that very much was happening; in fact, my life was rather dull. I've read that having a conversation like this is healing. For sure, I was sharing an adventure, dull as it was. (I quickly learned to be careful with these one-way conversations. One time when I started talking to you there were a lot of other people around. I noticed from the way they looked at me they thought I was a candidate for the "funny farm!")

But the little talks did help. I kept expecting you to talk back to me, but you never did. But I at least had someone to talk with, and you didn't argue with me.

Will my life ever be the same? No. However, I'm gradually discovering a new normalcy is possible, one that is defined differently than the one I had before with you. I won't forget you...ever. I decided a farewell ceremony of some kind is appropriate and would help. So I had one.

I will still grieve, but my life will not be dominated by grief.

You can't be replaced.

I can find love again.

One day as I was sitting at the desk in the study, looking at the pile of bills that had to be paid, I started opening drawers to look around. I really hadn't checked the desk thoroughly since your death. I found a partially-completed letter in the bottom right desk drawer. It was dated near the time we agreed there was a time coming when our partnership would end, but before you were in such terrible pain. Here's what it said:

My Darling,

I don't know how to write a letter like this. I got the idea from that "I'm Not Dead Yet" book, and thought it was a great thing to do. We'll see. This is my attempt to say some things that are for you and the family. Please share my thoughts with them. That book said it's good to read the letter out loud just before the will is shared, but do it whenever you choose.

We have tried to have a marriage that was based on mutual respect. I think we've done a pretty good job, don't you? Sharing good times and the bad (the bad was when the bills exceeded the income!) enabled us, early on, to understand the value of budgeting. We extended that idea and began making lists of things we wanted to do and then prioritizing them…usually first by how much the item would cost and then by how badly we wanted to do it. If a choice we were discussing ranked high on our list and we didn't have the money, we would start a saving account with the title of the project. Some project names come to mind: "Rome Trip," or "Santa Fe Weekend," or one I fondly remember, "Hotel Weekend." Do you remember that one? That little event resulted in our first born!

*We've shared Christian values. Service to others has
always been important, probably because we had so much joy
we wanted to pass on to others the values we treasured.*

*Your whole life has been my inspiration. I've tried to be
as loving and thoughtful as you, but I must admit you set a
pretty high standard. We've been blessed.*

*Now, when I know the end is in sight, I feel pretty good
about dying — though it's going to happen a lot sooner than
I would like. I truly believe God and I are going to be best
friends! It's the pain I dread; from what we've learned, there's
a lot of that coming. Thank God for pain killers!*

*My religious beliefs are based on the idea that people
are the result of past events , and they should live good lives
because they are the "past events" of the people who will live
in the future.*

*I never thought it was important to have a "firm" set
of beliefs. It was more important to me just to believe in
God and his love and not to quibble over the small points.
Our many discussions about evolution were events I looked
forward to. There are so many marvels in our universe and
some of them defy explanation...now. God's wisdom is being
revealed to us as we are capable of understanding. So there's
more to come!*

*A letter like this is to be shared (as I said earlier). So
these next paragraphs are for our sons.*

*You and I have done everything we could to instill family
values in our children, and I think we deserve a prize! They
all have loving relationships with their companions and their*

children. They have become successful businessmen, and they all are, each in their own unique way, making the world a better place. It is so wonderful it brings tears to my eyes.

We all know some people whose family life is dysfunctional. I feel sorry for them.

Our grandchildren and great grandchildren will be the smartest and most handsome and beautiful in the whole world! Absolutely!

It's always been easy for us to say to one another, "I love you," because it's true. I like to think the way you and I have lived our lives is spilling over to our kids — we all have a mutual respect for one another.

Aren't we lucky!

I'm going to have to stop soon, but before I end this writing session, forgiveness is a topic I want to mention. I will die without any hard feelings towards anyone. I forgive everybody! I hope anyone who has hard feelings for me will be able to put them aside after my death and remember only the good things (I do hope they can find some!).

The letter was put into the drawer and never finished. I wish I'd had it earlier; everyone would have benefitted from reading it. Even though it's incomplete, everyone in the family needs to have a copy. I'll make sure that happens.

What a love letter! Not known for being a literary person, your words came out in good form.

A "loving letter" is just what it was. Not too fluffy or macho; it obviously came from the heart. It was started, intended to be completed at a later date. I guess the disease galloped through and didn't pause long enough for you to finish it.

Sharing values, defining beliefs, expressing hope for survivors, expressing appreciation and love for those who are left, and telling a little of life's story (the good parts)—what more could one ask?

There's one more thing: a letter like this, incomplete as it was, sets the tone for all who read it. Appreciation, forgiveness, and love have been tattooed on my heart.

CHAPTER 16

DOLLARS

I WOKE UP with a start! Eyes wide open in a darkened bedroom. This waking panic is happening too often! The only light was the nightlight I had placed in the hall to keep from tripping when I got up at night to go to the bathroom. When did I start worrying about that?

What happened? What made me wake up? Was I going to be sick again? My heart was racing. I sat up in bed and then reached over to the nightstand to turn on a lamp.

Now, leaning against the headboard of the bed, I looked around. Nothing had changed. I was still alone. There was no other person in the room. The house wasn't on fire, and no pipes had broken, flooding the downstairs. There were no unusual noises.

Nothing.

I wasn't sick at my stomach.

What?

With the bedside light on, I slithered back into a prone position, pulled up the blankets, and shut my eyes. No good. Didn't work. I'm wide-awake. What time is it? The bedside clock glowed 2:19 a.m. Shall I try to go back to sleep? Watch TV? Read? Get up and do some work around the house? That last question was the first to receive a resounding "No."

Think.

Ah ha...I didn't remember.

Think some more.

Finally, I got a flash. I'm worried about the bank account and insurance. I guess the reason it didn't immediately pop into my head is that there's money in the bank; the insurance company had sent me a check. OK, in spite of assurances and cash, I'm worried. Don't know why. So what do I do about it at 2:21 am.?

I reached over, turned off the lamp, and snuggled back under the covers....

When you have someone to discuss financial decisions with, especially if something goes wrong, it's comforting to be able to say, "Well this is a decision we made together, so you made a mistake, too." Now I didn't have anyone to join me in the "buck stops here." It was all me.

Were there decisions to be made that involved substantial risk? No, none that I knew of.

What is it?

I worried about it a while longer. I really didn't know what specifically to worry about, but I tried. When you're wide-awake in a darkened room, it's easy just to lay there and wonder about the future.

After a while, I went back to sleep.

That's another problem solved...for now.

CHAPTER 17

WHAT HAPPENED TO ROMANCE?

THE EMOTIONS ASSOCIATED with love are described from a unique perspective in romance novels. From a real world assessment, they're unreal. In the fictional story, it seems every hero is young, muscular, handsome, rich, an intellectual, socially sophisticated, protective, and, finally, a giant in bed.

Every heroine is beautiful, slim, curvaceous, ample-breasted, has shiny, wavy hair, is able to make her own way in the world and, yes, she's sexy. In addition to her physical appearance, she has brains, gorgeous clothes, a fabulous house (or castle), wealth, parents who understand her (or don't, depending on the plot), and a brother or friend who is the villain.

Check the people walking in the shopping malls. That's reality!

I had been widowed long enough that there would be no gossip if I started dating. I treasure the memories of my marriage, but had convinced myself that you would not want me to spend the rest of my life alone. I was ready.

Middle-aged romance is a little more practical than a youngster's idea of finding a companion. I am middle-aged, so I ought to know. Right?

When you're past 50 and believe you're ready for another chance at love, you're very careful of the next-person-standards you set.

After all, you may not be a catch yourself. For many, the search begins with a weight-loss program and physical conditioning. Some of us depend on surgery for help. I'd like to have a nip here and a tuck there if I could afford it. There are a few places on my body that would benefit from a plastic surgeon's skills.

For the last few months I had been exercising, slowly at first and never at the fever pitch some of the younger ones at my gym did. I was religious about following an exercise regimen, although I backslid occasionally. But I kept at it. After I'd been on this "new you" routine a while, I concluded I hadn't felt this good in years! It was a hard road to get there, but I'm glad I did.

What next? Am I really ready for the next step?

Yes. I'm ready.

Where would I go to meet my new person? A bar? A gym? On the golf course? As a volunteer? A discussion group? An on-line singles connection? In a church? In a singles Sunday School class?

This list sounds familiar. These are the same places I thought about when I was in "recovery" mode. But now I try to think of myself as more aggressive, more ready, and, frankly, better looking.

Maybe I'll depend on my friends fixing me up with someone they know is "right" for me.

All the approaches work. Maybe they all won't work for me, but one will. So, I'll try one, and if I don't make a good connection, I'll try another. I'm not going to give up my trying for romance. My marriage was too good not to want to repeat that experience.

Wow!

After looking at myself naked in front of a full size mirror, I've discovered that, because of my new physical appearance and, especially, my new attitude, I need a more stylish wardrobe. This decision took a chunk of time from my full-speed ahead program and my check book, but I considered it essential. Getting new outfits was fun, but expensive. I hoped it was worth it.

Times have changed since I last participated in a courtship and romance relationship, so there are rules to learn. I can learn them by trial and error or get advice from someone who's been down the trail.

This is an important time in my new life. I need to plan entry into the world of dating and romance. I wondered how you'd feel about what I am doing? The more I considered it, the more I became convinced my dead husband would agree it was a good thing to be doing.

I mentally wished myself, "Good luck!"

Here I am, in bed, watching a "chick flick." (It doesn't make any difference whether you're a man or a woman—there are some times you watch what's on the tube whether you want to or not. In your mind, you just decide it's something to do.)

Here it comes: The passionate embrace. The kiss, followed by a shot of the wind blowing the curtains, or the waves breaking on the shore. You have to imagine what has happened. (You can tell this is an old movie— these days they don't leave hardly anything to your imagination. It's a kiss, then off with their clothes and into the bed. They roll around a lot, grind hips and then lean back against the pillows and display what's supposed to be the contented look of "did the world move for you, too?")

Today, after sex, the movies don't show couples lying in bed smoking cigarettes. They do show sweaty bodies!

The credits start rolling up the screen. Did I go to sleep? Was I daydreaming? Am I finally capable of thinking that romance is possible? What's happening?

I fluff up the bed pillow and try to settle in. How long have I been without my partner? Can I now say, "How long have I been without my 'lover?' without flinching?" I'm trying.

I'm wide awake now. Recently I've thought about things I haven't thought about for a long, long time. I've convinced myself that my decision to move on was right. It's time to get serious about starting a new life. It's time to consider these things without feeling guilty.

OK. I'll try. What do I do first?

Well, to begin, go back to sleep. It's a little after midnight, not a good time to start looking for adventure. Start tomorrow.

It's 6 a.m. That's one thing that hasn't changed; I still wake up too early. My routine is to put my feet on the floor, go to the bathroom, and then put on the coffee. Go get the paper. I've decided that it's with the paper the changing will start. I won't do the crosswords, yet, I'll read the funnies first. Then cereal. That's the same as always.

I'm on my second cup of coffee. The paper is laid out on the kitchen table. Is there a section for people who want to get started on a new life? Probably not. It seems several companies have ads for THE solution, and it only costs $150, payable in two easy installments.

Is one of those "Single" organizations the answer? I've been through these mental gymnastics before, and I'm doing it again. There are groups for every taste: Christian Singles and Mature Singles are places to start. I'll also call that gal at church who coordinates the Singles Group (I'll give it another try!). I might try one of these computer matching companies I see advertising on TV. And, not my last choice, but close to last, there's always a bar.

See, I'm trying.

Wait. How about my shopping cart friend? We're due to get together for coffee soon. I'll discuss my decision with her; maybe she has some good advice.

CHAPTER 18

WAGONS HO!
ON THE TRAIL AGAIN

THAT'S HOW THEY do it in the Westerns. The Wagon Master lines up all the wagons, followed by the people on horses, and then those on foot. Waving one arm, he shouts, "Wagons Ho." Or, at least, he yells something that is supposed to indicate a new adventure is starting. Several of the horse riders fall behind the walkers, protecting the rear against the bad guys, or I guess I should say, "Indians."

As I get out of my car in the shopping center parking lot, I raise one arm to the sky and say, under my breath, "Giddy up."

A Starbucks straight or in any flavor is always a pick-me-up. After a couple of swallows, caffeine coursing through my body, my mind starts racing. Where my mind is going, I don't yet know. Time to send up a trial balloon.

My friend, Ruth, was a little late, so my cup was about empty when she arrived. After an apology, she got us both a latte. A second jolt would have me climbing the walls, but I drank it anyway. Ruth and I had become fast friends since we first met in the vegetable aisle at the local supermarket, so there's not a lot of small talk before we get right into whatever is on our minds. I was first to speak.

"I think I've finally turned the corner," was my opening salvo to my friend. "Getting back into the real world no longer seems like an issue that can't be faced. I believe I'm ready."

After taking a swig of my latte, I continued with, "I know you're way ahead of me in this 're-entry' thing. How're you doing?"

She did her habitual hand to her hair, giving her graying hair a little flip. That was the signal she really did have something to say. I sat there, waiting.

"Fat and fifty doesn't scare off all the guys. I've found one who is interested in me for more than my fabulous figure," said the slightly overweight citizen sitting across from me.

"Really?" The word in the form of a question was my invitation to her to tell me more. "And don't leave out any of the juicy parts."

"We met, of all places, in a neighborhood bar," Ruth said as her story started to unfold. "My girlfriend, Sally, was visiting me. I was out of wine so I suggested we go up the street to a bar that had been in the neighborhood for years.

"We walked in. The lights were low and the 'regulars' were seated at the bar having the usual conversations about sports, and, probably, women. We got a table and, after a reasonable wait, two glasses of House Red showed up.

"We toasted each other and began girl talk. I had just gotten a sentence or two out of my mouth when this guy walks up to the table and says to me, 'I think I live down the street from you. Do you remember me?'

"I thought it was a legitimate question, not a come-on line, so I looked him squarely in the eyes. Sure enough, I recognized him."

From this point on, Ruth told the story as if it were happening in real time; she was re-living each moment.

I said, "Aren't you the Bob that is married to Jean? And I do remember that you live down the street from us. I still live in my house."

"Bob's reply to my question was, 'Yes. " He then started bringing me up to date with the things that had happened in his life the last couple of years. He said, "I was married to Jean until about a year and a-half ago. She ran into her high school sweetheart and decided living with him would be more fun than living with me. She's gone, and we're divorced." He told me his former wife's new husband is everything he wasn't, particularly that the guy is seriously rich. He said, "He's loaded, and I'm just a working stiff." Then, with a mischievous grin, said, "He's fat."

He stood there, waiting for an invitation to join us. I didn't get the chance to make that suggestion before my table companion, Sally, said, "So you're a neighbor. And you're divorced?"

With that easy question, he pulled out a chair and sat down. "Yes. She left me with the house, the mortgage, the dog and cat, and two boys. The boys are both in college now and seem to be pretty well adjusted. And the mortgage has about five more years to run.

"Until recently, I've been on the road trying to get my little company established. I've been living out of a suitcase for, it seems like, forever. 'Not at home much. That's why I'm unsure about who my neighbors are."

Ruth said, "With that, he turned to me and said, "What's happened to you in the years since Jean left me?"

"I told him my husband had died, that he had Parkinson's and that his last years were very difficult." She paused to take a breath before continuing.

Taking advantage of the pause, my friend, Sally, jumped back into the conversation, trying to establish her own beachhead with the visitor, "I'm divorced, too. I went back to college, got my degree, and went to work, in that order. My hubby left me for a small waist, big breasts, a fancy car, and, he said, great sex."

There was a long pause. Bob didn't acknowledge her disclosures, and neither did I.

Ignoring her and looking directly at me, Bob continued, "Well, it sounds like all our ships burned at sea." After a short pause, still ignoring the 'small waist, big breasts' commentator, he smiled, looked into my eyes, and said, "Have you re-entered the social scene yet?"

"This question ignited the atmosphere," said Ruth, her eyes sparkling. "There was instant rapport between the two of us. I think the air was smoking!"

She continued, "Before I could reply to the social scene question, my friend re-entered the conversation and answered the question for me.

"She was just telling me she's ready." As Sally said this, there was this big smile on her face and an impish look in her eyes. She had given up trying to be a part of the ritual and had gone over to my side, trying to do what she could to help."

Bob picked up from there. Striking as handsome a pose as possible, he looked at me and said, "I'd like to learn more about your transition. May I take you to dinner tomorrow night, Ruth?"

Returning to reality and to her enthralled listener, she leaned back in her chair, sighed, then said, "We went to dinner, and now we're racing along the romance trail. I'm not sure where it's going, but I love it so far." Waxing poetic, she said, "I think we're headed for the moon." She sighed again, got a far-off gaze in her eyes before putting the finale to one of the nicest romance stories I'd ever heard, "I think there's a chance for me, yet."

I leaned over the table, looked her in the eyes, and said, "Have you had sex yet?"

She just smiled. Question answered.

"Well," I said. "Congratulations. Just one more question: why was he in a bar in the middle of the afternoon?"

"You know," Ruth replied, "I've never asked."

We continued talking and gossiping. She didn't mention her visiting girlfriend any more, and I didn't ask about her. But her confession was the tonic I needed. My decision to "jump in" was reinforced. I was going to do it.

CHAPTER 19

THE RIGHT PEW

LIFE PLAYED A trick on me. As the months rolled by, I was about recovered from the death of my husband when my mother became ill. I took care of her for months until she died. I was the sibling that made all the final arrangements.

As I sat on a hard wooden pew in the small-town church where my mother's funeral was about to begin, the events of the recent and so long ago past came flooding into my mind. It's funny: I now am able to remember my husband's death without tears. I still miss him, but I had crossed a threshold of some kind.

I looked at the small group of people sitting in the pews; they were the last of her old-time friends. She and this small circle had outlived what was once a large mixture of both men and women. The ones left were gathered to pay their last respects and to recall memories. She and my dad had lived in the same town and the same house since their marriage.

I sat there in the pew, trying to think my way through the days and months ahead. My mother's death was a struggle; she was glad when the end came. I agreed. She lived a good life. I had done everything I could to make her last days comfortable. I knew her rewards in heaven were coming. I missed her comments about the "good old days," and the friendly advice she gave without asking. There were lots of things to think about.

But, I wasn't able to put into concrete what I was going to

do now. I discovered my best intentions couldn't compete with old-fashioned luck.

It's funny, the way fate treats you. Like my friend who met her new soul mate in a bar. She would never have guessed when she went into the neighborhood hangout that events would unfold that eventually gave her a chance at romance and a happy life.

Her unplanned encounter was not the only one with a happy ending. This next chapter of my life is like a fairy tale.

As I said, I was sitting in a church pew reminiscing about my mother's life. What happened next illustrates perfectly how unexpected happenings sometimes just come along, right out of the blue, and your life is never the same.

My encounter with good luck started at my mother's funeral.

The sequence of events will never be re-told by romance journalists or make it into any books of witty experiences, but the things that happened next were a life changer for me.

Grief turned out to be my path to romance.

As the funeral service started, I didn't notice any more the hardness of the pew where I sat. I guess my rear end had gone numb.

This was the funeral of my dearest friend, my mother. She finally had lost her long battle with cancer. She had fought and fought until finally her body just wore out. She had been so supportive when my husband was in the last horrible phase of his cancer. Losing her was another blow to my fragile existence. Cancer had struck down the two most important people in my life.

As I thought about the past, the hurt was intense. I listened to the minister recount my mother's life, and, as I thought about my parent's long marriage, anguish filled me. It was hard to breathe.

The memories came flooding back. Always supportive, Mother rehearsed me as I prepared for school plays. She sat closest to the stage during the performance and clapped loudest when the play ended. She was the one who held a box of tissues while listening to me tell about my first romance and my heartbreak when it ended. She even comforted me at my father's death.

When I left for college, she encouraged me in every letter or phone call.

My marriage was a "happiest event ever" for her. Later, she suffered with me in my personal tragedy. She had prayed for me my entire life.

When her illness was diagnosed, I was the logical family member to take care of her. I was alone; I had no emotional commitments that would keep me away. My sister had a wonderful new baby, and my brother had recently married his childhood sweetheart; they were still in the honeymoon phase of their marriage. Single me was the right one to be the caregiver. Among my siblings, as the female child without entanglements since my husband's untimely death, I did the right thing. I counted caring for our mother an honor.

The minister spoke on with the funeral sermon. "OK, Lord, what's next?" I mentally asked. My life stretched out before me as an empty canvass, eagerly waiting for the first stroke of a paintbrush. For a moment, I was actually frightened as I contemplated life without my husband and now, my mother. My dad had been dead a long time, so life had already filled that void. I looked at my brother who sat stoically with his face toward the minister. He was clutching his wife's hand. My sister sat slumped against her husband's shoulder, his arm around her as she cradled their sleeping child. All were deeply grieving and lost in their private thoughts. No one noticed I sat alone.

My chosen place had been with my gravely ill mother, preparing her meals, helping her walk, taking her to the doctor, seeing to her many, many pills. I read to her; her favorites were Zane Grey western novels and the Old Testament. Early in her illness, we read the Bible together; I would read one chapter and she would read the next. Now she was with the Lord. My caregiving work was finished. I was alone...again.

Lost in my reveries, I heard a door open and slam shut at the back of the church. Quick footsteps hurried along; I imagined the walker trying to float over the carpet so his arrival would be inconspicuous. It wasn't possible; his steps made too much noise in a small church.

The person walked up the aisle until he was next to me. I looked at him: an exasperated man, confused and anxious. He paused, looked around, and then sat next to me. I had quickly scooted over to make room for him. He folded his arms, frowned, obviously out of sorts at being late.

I could tell he was upset about arriving after the service had already begun. He seemed sadder than most of the other non-family attending the service. His eyes were brimming with tears as he removed a handkerchief from his pocket and blew his nose. He began to sniffle. "I'm late," he explained, though no explanation was necessary. His late entrance was impossible to ignore; the whole church was aware of it.

The sermon ended; a local woman sang one of Mom's favorite hymns, and the eulogies by friends and loved ones began.

After several persons had spoken, he leaned over and commented, "I knew Mary quite well; why do they keep calling her 'Margaret?'"

"Because that was her name, 'Margaret.' No one ever called her 'Mary,'" I whispered.

Who was this person who came to the funeral of a person he knew well enough to grieve for, but didn't know her name? I wished to myself that he had sat on the other side of the church or in one of several empty pews. I was no longer the solitary mourner on my row; he had interrupted my grieving with his demeanor, his tears and questions. Now he had asked a question that didn't make sense.

"No, that isn't correct," he insisted, as several people glanced over at us, obviously wishing us to be quiet. "Her name is Mary, Mary Peters. It always has been 'Mary'."

"That isn't who this is."

"Isn't this the Presbyterian church?"

"No, the Presbyterian church is across the street. This is the Lutheran Church."

"Oh."

"I believe you're at the wrong funeral, and in the wrong pew," I responded, getting a little jab in at the way he had entered the church and chose my row to sit in.

Then, without warning, I understood what had happened. His grief, the solemnness of the occasion, followed by the comprehension of his mistake; all that information bubbled up inside me and came out as laughter. I put my handkerchief over my face, trying to muffle my laughter and at the same time hoping everyone would interpret my interruption as sobs of grief. The creaking pew gave me away. Ugly looks from other mourners only made the situation worse— but funnier. The bewildered, misguided man seated beside me was laughing too. He glanced around; deciding as I had that it was too late for an uneventful exit. We both sat, able at last to remain silent.

At the final "Amen," we left with the others, after shaking hands with the minister.

As we went towards the parked cars, he said, "Well, this was a funeral I won't forget!" followed by a chuckle and a smile. He said, "Since I've missed my aunt's funeral, what am I going to do?" He answered his own question by inviting me to join him for a cup of coffee.

That afternoon, over pie and coffee, I passed from grief to a new beginning. A chance encounter at the least likely of events began a lifelong, loving journey for me with this man. He attended the wrong funeral, yes, but he was where he should have been.

Ours was a storybook romance, filled with all the courtship events lovers could imagine. Over the next ten months, we discovered many shared interests, a similar upbringing, and shared a strong faith. When he asked me to marry him, he did it on the balcony of a lovely inn, with the sun setting and casting a rosy glow over everything.

We married, the second time for both of us, The ceremony was at the country Presbyterian Church he attended. This time there was no confusion about where to go or what time the ceremony would take place. We both arrived at the right church, right on time.

Our new home would be his house. I had sold mine; it had too many memories to overcome. My children had grown to know their new dad well. It was an easy transition for the kids. They were happy to have an adult male in their lives again.

In my time of sorrow, my pain and grief were swept away. After months of confusion and doubt, I found love again, along with the joy and laughter my life needed. In place of the loneliness that had been my companion, was a best friend and lover. Our meeting was a miracle.

Whenever anyone asks how we met, we tell them, "My mother and his Aunt Mary introduced us." What we don't often say to others, but both of us believe, is ours was a match made in heaven.

What a wonderful story. Wouldn't it be great if every story had a happy ending?

God, I need you.
Carry me when I'm weak;
Hold me when I'm tired.
Love me when I cannot care
     anymore.
And when I huddle lonely
     and afraid, cover me
     with your strong,
     protective hands.
Guard my sleep, and wake
     me in the morning,
     rested and strong,
     and ready to try again.

Author unknown

www.ingramcontent.com/pod-product-compliance
Lightning Source LLC
Chambersburg PA
CBHW031321040426
42443CB00005B/179